Oral and Written Communication

By the same author

Communication in Business
English for the Office

Oral and Written Communication

Peter Little

Head of the Department of
Office Studies and General Education,
The College, Swindon.

Longman

LONGMAN GROUP LIMITED
London

Associated companies, branches and representatives
throughout the world

© Longman Group Limited 1973

First published 1973

ISBN 0 582 42225.6

Set in IBM Press Roman 9 on 10 pt.

and Printed in Great Britain
by William Clowes & Sons Limited, London, Colchester and Beccles.

Contents

Preface: for teachers

Oral and Written Communication aims to provide an introduction to communication principles combined with a revision course in language. It is intended for class use with young people who found conventional English classes at school rather heavy going but whose work will demand some ability in verbal communication, especially face-to-face communication with customers and clients.

The kind of young person I have had in mind in preparing it is the one who is going to be a sales assistant, a hairdresser, a receptionist, a waiter or waitress etc. Many potential users of this book will already be employed as juniors (in distribution or hairdressing, for example) and attending a college of further education on part-time release. Others will be on full-time college courses leading to trade qualifications. Others will still be at school (for I hope *Oral and Written Communication* will prove useful during the ROSLA year with pupils who are likely, on leaving, to take up jobs involving serving customers.) To avoid tedious repetition of such phrases as 'or your school' I have written throughout as if all users are at college, relying on teachers to make the necessary minor adaptations when the book is used in school.

I started out with a much more limited aim – to write a textbook for students on day release from the distributive trades following the compulsory Oral and Written Communication syllabus in the General Certificate in Distribution. This is still the primary function of *Oral and Written Communication*; but it seemed worth while to broaden the approach sufficiently to make it suitable for other groups of students with similar communication needs in their work and, probably, similar weaknesses in their control of language.

Widening the job spectrum of those who would use the book accentuated a problem that was already there anyhow (since 'distribution' itself incorporates an enormous range of jobs) – how to provide applications, illustrations, and exercises that were felt to be relevant to their work by all. My policy over this has been to try to give most potential users a turn but to draw the bulk of my examples from retailing, since everybody has some knowledge of shops and stores, if only as an occasional customer. Where a teacher is fortunate enough to be taking a class all of whom have the same trade background he will not find it difficult to adapt my retailing applications to ones relevant to that particular trade if he thinks this desirable. I do, however, think it is important that teachers stress early in the course that it is the principle involved that matters, not the specific illustration of it. It cannot possibly be the function of a textbook (or a teacher) to supply models for every communication situation that students are likely to meet in their work.

The majority of those for whom this book is intended will have little, or no, need to write at work. Their interest in improving their skill in written communication will be maintained only if this is presented as a necessary attribute of successful living outside work. Future promotion to supervisory level may well depend on ability to communicate in writing adequately – but this is a consideration that will influence only the tiny minority who see promotion as a feasible target.

What is an immediate vocational need of almost all such students (and they are usually well aware of this) is to improve their oral communication standard. There is a limit to what the writer of the textbook can do here – the class teacher's role is of paramount importance. It is important that as much as possible of the material should be treated orally, especially in the early stages. To this end I have cut back on exposition and written exercises and substituted, whenever possible, class discussion and group activity. I am counting on teachers to supply the sort of material that I cannot: local and/or topical newspaper cuttings; tape recordings of radio broadcasts; short films; where a VTR is available, video-recordings – anything of this kind that will stimulate lively and informed discussion.

As the General Certificate in Distribution course is normally a two-year one I have divided my material into two parts. Where only one year is available for a communication course it will be necessary to run the two parts together as neither is complete in itself.

With students who are preparing for the National Distribution Certificate on the three-year scheme *Oral and Written Communication* will be found satisfactory for the first two years but should be supplemented by Little, *Communication in Business* (2nd edition, Longman 1970) for the final year.

I have given some thought to the order in which material is presented to the student and have endeavoured to keep the course progressive. I find that a recurring criticism of school English courses made by FE students is that these are repetitive and non-progressive. To use the book as I intend, all chapters except 9 and 12 should be studied in the order in which they appear, with perhaps the occasional exercise held back to be used later for revision purposes. Some of the practice work in Chapter 9 may be introduced as soon as Chapter 6 is completed. The material for practice in receiving communication in Chapter 12 is arranged in ascending order of difficulty and it is intended that the more difficult practice work should be introduced from time to time, to give variety, during the later stages of the course. Spelling rules appear as an appendix so that these can be introduced when the teacher requires them. Metrication and postcoding are also the subjects of appendices, the intention being that students refer to these themselves when they find a need to do so.

PETER LITTLE

Acknowledgements

We are grateful to the following for permission to reproduce copyright material:

Collins Publishers for an extract from *The Neophilliacs* by Christopher Booker; The *Daily Telegraph* for Gerda Paul's article, Deterioration of food standards from the *Daily Telegraph Magazine*, 4.6.71, James Mitchell's article from the *Daily Telegraph Magazine*, 4.12.70, Fenton Bresler's article from the *Daily Telegraph Magazine*, 4.6.71 and Geo Hubbard for use of his letter to the *Daily Telegraph*, 4.6.71; Post Office for use of the *Post Office Alphabet*; Penguin Books Ltd for an adapted extract from *Your Money's Worth* by Elizabeth Gundrey; *The Sunday Times* for an extract from *The Sunday Times Magazine*, 11.10.70 article by Peter Laurie dealing with dangers of driving; The Treasury for a table from the Treasury Broadsheet on Britain No. 3, *Consumer Spending*; Union of Educational Institutions for Question 3 of June, 1970 Examination, *Certificate in Retailing* and Ward Lock Educational Ltd for an extract from *Wool* by P. A. Wells.

We are unable to trace the copyright holders of the letters from *Which?* magazine and would appreciate receiving any information that would enable us to do so.

We are grateful to the following for permission to reproduce illustrations and photographs:

Dunlop Ltd for page 48; Newcastle Evening Chronicle for page 58; Dunn and Co. for pages 60–61; Sport and General for page 62; Technical Development Capital Ltd for page 63 (bottom); The Daily Telegraph for page 63 (top); Herbert Bayer for page 64; J. M. Dent and Son Ltd for page 65; The Local Government Information Office for England and Wales for pages 66–67; Rosenthal/Heals for page 68; Daily Mirror for page 74; Parkray Ltd for page 112; Thistle Hotels Ltd for page 114; Associated Newspapers/Weekend for page 124; The Observer for page 126.

The author wishes to express his gratitude to Mrs Norma Dobie for preparing the typescript and to his wife for reading proofs.

NOTE. The names and addresses of individuals, firms and organisations used in examples and exercises in this book are fictitious. Any resemblance to the name and address of an existing individual, firm, or organisation is coincidental.

These fictitious addresses have been arbitrarily allocated postcodes which may in fact be the postcodes of existing areas or even specific addresses but which for the purpose of this book refer only to the fictitious addresses.

Only in work and through work do living human beings have much to say to each other.

Ernst Fischer

Part One

1
Introduction

You are starting a two-year course in communication. We had better make sure right from the start that you know what we mean by *communication*.

Like most words, *communication* has, in fact, a number of meanings. As used in this book it refers to the ways in which we get in touch with each other – how we show each other our feelings; tell each other our thoughts; ask questions; ask for help; pass on facts; argue; persuade others to do what we want them to do; explain; give orders. We all spend a very large part of our waking lives communicating. Although in this book we are particularly concerned with improving communication at work, effective communication is also vital to us in our private lives. The more effective we are as communicators, the more effective we are as human beings.

The term *Communication* (with a capital *C*) is used as the name of a subject for study (compare *Mathematics, Economics*). It is quite a new subject, one that has been studied only in the period since the Second World War. It is concerned with the methods we use in communicating with each other and how we can improve our use of these. The term *Oral and Written Communication*, used as the title of this book, refers only to one part of the Communication field – communicating by means of speech and writing. (There are, of course, many other ways of communicating.)

Some sort of human communication must have been going on ever since the first recognisably human creatures developed on this planet, but millions of years passed before man invented speech. Communication by speech has probably existed for something approaching 500 000 years. Communication by writing is a more recent invention; it has been in use for only about 5000 years. In view of the long time human beings have been communicating with each other it seems odd that it is only in the second half of the twentieth century that we have started to look in some detail at what we do when we communicate, and begun to think about how we can do it more effectively.

Oral and written communication, although it is a new subject, will not seem all that unfamiliar to you. After all, you have probably been communicating by speech since you were two years old and by writing since you were about six. In English classes at school you will already have

3

come across all the fundamentals of using our language that we shall be looking at again from a communication viewpoint on this course.

Communication (especially oral communication) plays a very big part in the work of sales assistants, hairdressers, waiters and waitresses, hotel receptionists etc. and it is for young men and girls in such work (or expecting to take up such work) that this book is intended. Improving your skill in oral and written communication is not, however, just something that will make you more efficient in your job – it affects your whole life outside work as well.

What can you personally gain from following a course like this? The aim is twofold:

1. To widen your communication range
2. To improve your effectiveness as a communicator.

Let us look at these points more closely for a moment – first 'to widen your communication range'. You probably communicate as effectively as the next chap* with your mate at work, your girl friend etc. – those who know you pretty well, are of about your age, and have similar backgrounds to you. But how do you make out with customers? the boss? your girl friend's father? your own parents? Again, you may get by when you only have to *talk* to people. But what sort of a shot would you make at a business letter, or a report arising from your claim on the company insuring your scooter?

As for improving your effectiveness as a communicator – are you really completely satisfied that you always communicate to others just what you want to communicate? Or are you sometimes puzzled because they do not seem to understand you properly? Do you get mixed up when you try to explain something you know a good deal about to somebody who knows very little about it? Can you use words in such a way as to produce exactly the kind of response you want from other people? Do you find it difficult to put your ideas into words? Can you put your ideas down on paper? When you write a letter to a firm do you get the sort of action you expect? Do they ignore your letters altogether or write asking you to give further details? Do firms you write to make mysterious mistakes in dealing with your letters?

You will probably be willing to agree without any more self-questioning that there is plenty of room for improvement in your communication skills and that a course in oral and written communication which may help to reduce communication breakdowns of the kind hinted at in the last two paragraphs will be of value to you in private life as well as at work.

---

* This book is intended for both sexes, but where references would have to be duplicated to refer to both, the reader is assumed to be masculine.

2
What Communication is All About

I. Defining communication

Start by rereading the second paragraph of Chapter 1. If we use the word 'information' rather broadly we could call all the communication activities mentioned in that paragraph 'information passing'. 'Information passing' also includes asking for information. You might say that when we ask for a piece of information we are passing on the information that we lack that piece of information.

For a 'communication situation' to exist the information must be passed (or *transmitted* we usually say) for a purpose. We may wish to make somebody (1) act in a certain way (or stop acting in a certain way), or (2) change his attitude towards us or somebody else, or (3) change his attitude towards some object or idea (this is how we get people to buy what we want them to buy, for example). In short, we want a 'response'.

We can get a response from people by telling them lies; by threatening them with a weapon; by prodding them in a tender part with a sharpened stick. These are not the kinds of response we aim at with our communication skills. From communication we expect a response based on understanding the facts. It is possible, for example, to sell a customer an item by describing it falsely, or incompletely, or by giving false information about rival products. If we are selling by communication, we pass on all the information we have that we think the customer will find useful in making up his mind. The sale results from the customer's choosing logically (or as logically as he can, for most people are not very logical) on the basis of the information put before him. The sale is then a response based on understanding the information transmitted – an 'understanding response'.

It should be made clear immediately that this is not to be taken as meaning that all communication is *intentional* communication. It is quite possible to communicate accidentally or unconsciously – even against the communicator's wishes – and for a response to result that the communicator did not desire at all. An obvious example is when we are frightened but try our best to disguise this from other people by what we say and the way we say it. Very often our fear is quite clearly communicated (by facial expression, pallor, tenseness of body) despite all our efforts.

Unconscious communication of this kind can be very important in dealing with customers. A sales assistant, for example, may—while saying all the right things about the product—at the same time antagonise the customer by strong unconscious communication (by tone of voice, facial expression, body posture) which virtually says: 'I am bored to death with you and the product.'

It is not only individuals who communicate. Organisations (for example: shops, stores, wholesalers, restaurants, hotels, colleges, civil service departments) also communicate, both with each other and with individuals. Our sales assistant is communicating not only as an individual but also as a representative of the store that employs him. His unconscious communication of a bored attitude may therefore produce a very undesirable response: the customer may develop an attitude of antagonism not only towards this particular assistant but towards the whole store. In other words the assistant may not just lose that one sale, he may lose the store a customer.

Putting all these points together, we can now attempt a simple definition of *communication*.

Communication is the process by which information is transmitted between individuals and/or organisations so that an understanding response results.

II. The communication process

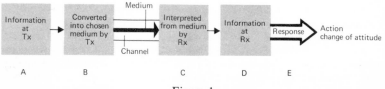

Figure 1.

Figure 1 represents the communication process. For convenient reference, we can name the person who is transmitting the information the 'Transmitter' (abbreviation Tx) and the person or persons to whom the transmission is directed the 'Receiver' (abbreviation Rx).

If we lived in a science fiction world where we all practised telepathy we would not have to bother with a 'medium'. We would simply think our message hard and it would form in the mind of the receiver. Unfortunately (or perhaps fortunately – who wants to be reading other people's minds all day long?) real life is not like this. We need a medium to carry our message. The medium that concerns us in this book is words but there are many other *media* (note this plural) for conveying information from one human being to another.

The 'channel' connects Tx to Rx. It is the path through which the medium moves or the situation that permits the Tx to communicate with the Rx. If you communicate by letter the channel is the mailing system of the Post Office. If you are speaking you may use a telephone for a long-distance channel. The communication channel used by teachers is the timetabling system of the college which ensures that the class and teacher go to the same classroom at the same time, so that communication can take place. (This is a part of the communication system of colleges that often breaks down at the beginning of a session. No communication can take place at all if the teacher has been sent to Room 53 but the class to Room 35.) The channel for a sales assistant is the selling situation which brings assistant and customer face-to-face in store or shop, and similar channels exist between hairdresser and client, waiter and diner etc.

For the response at E in Figure 1 to be exactly what the Tx hoped for, communication must be perfect. For perfect communication the information at D must be identical with that at A. In practice this is very difficult to achieve because of distortion at B and C. When the Tx puts his ideas into the medium he may misrepresent his ideas through lack of skill in using the medium even though the ideas are clear enough in his head. Similarly the Rx may misinterpret the medium, bringing in a second level of distortion. Clearly, the more both Tx and Rx know about how to use the chosen medium the less the distortion will be and the nearer to perfection the operation of the communication process.

In distribution, and such jobs as hairdressing and waiting, by far the most important communication medium is our own language. The more you know about using words the more useful you will be as a communicator in this sort of work.

Although there are circumstances where communication is bound to be oneway (reading a book for example) the best communication is twoway. Of course, in many communication situations, especially face-to-face communication by means of spoken words, the parties concerned take it in turns to be Tx and Rx. (We sometimes refer to this as a 'dialogue'.) This is often, for example, the situation between sales assistant and customer. In other circumstances the Tx may stay in that role for a considerable time and the Rx's contribution is confined perhaps to a few questions. A lecturer instructing a class is a clear example of this; but a sales assistant may find himself in a similar situation if, for example, he has to give a long explanation of the way some appliance he is selling works.

The bad communicator is one who in a dialogue situation resents losing the Tx role and will not give the Rx a chance to become Tx for more than a few moments. He goes on talking all the time himself, or interrupts the other man as soon as he has uttered a few words. Similarly when circumstances are of the kind where the Tx is bound to maintain that role for a considerable time, the bad communicator takes no notice of how the Rx is receiving what he is trying to communicate and gives him no chance to ask questions or otherwise indicate his reaction to the information transmitted.

We call this reaction from the Rx 'feedback'. Ideally feedback should be so rapid that the Tx can immediately adjust what he is transmitting to fit the feedback. Thus if a sales assistant in a department store is explaining the differences between reel-to-reel and cassette tape recorders and the customer begins to look puzzled, the assistant can immediately adjust by going more slowly or perhaps repeating what he has been saying in a simpler form. In face-to-face communication the opportunities for feedback are excellent. Over a telephone it is more difficult as you have to give the Rx a chance to say something before you know how he is taking what you are saying. Feedback to written communication is slow. If you write a letter to somebody that annoys him or that he cannot understand, you have to wait for him to write back (or come storming into your place of work) to find out his reaction. You may never find it out – you may have lost a customer without ever knowing why.

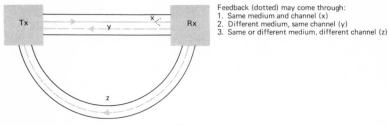

Feedback (dotted) may come through:
1. Same medium and channel (x)
2. Different medium, same channel (y)
3. Same or different medium, different channel (z)

Figure 2.

Figure 2 illustrates feedback. Feedback need not be by means of the same medium as that used by the Tx. Our example about the tape recorders illustrates feedback through facial expression while the Tx was using spoken words. It may not even be through the same channel. The customer who receives a letter he does not like and comes into the shop to complain provides an example of this.

For discussion
1. How do you imagine primitive man communicated before he had invented language?
2. What disadvantages would there be to having a spoken language without a written language? (Man must have been in that situation for hundreds of thousands of years.)
3. How many media of communication can you think of that do not rely on words (i.e. 'non-verbal media')?
4. How many examples of channels of communication can you think of?
5. What kinds of feedback operate when a lecturer is instructing a class in college?

III. Communication situations

A communication situation does not necessarily exist just because words (or some other medium of communication) are being used. We use the media of communication for purposes other than communication, of which the most important is *expression*. Poets, painters, composers are obvious examples; but ordinary people also use the media of communi-cations just to express their feelings for their own satisfaction. What about swearing, for example? Again, words may be used for no other purpose than to establish contact with somebody or perhaps open up a channel of communication if we have information to pass on. When we say 'Hello!' to somebody or 'Nice day!' we are not communicating; we are merely making friendly noises that may be a prelude to communication or may be complete in themselves, just tiny gestures of goodwill.

Let us imagine a situation. A man and a girl are leaning on a parapet watching the sun setting over the sea. It is not very clear to you from the way they are standing whether they know one another well or not, or even if they know each other at all. As you go by, you hear the man say: 'What a beautiful sunset!'

From the evidence before you the situation can be interpreted four ways.

1. It is *not a communication situation at all*. The man is simply using words to express his feelings about the sunset. The fact that somebody else is there is not of much importance to him, although he would probably not have voiced his thoughts aloud if he had been alone. He is not attempting to pass on information about the sunset and to obtain a response from the girl.
2. Some *unconscious communication* may result if they have previously known each other. The man's motive in speaking may be the same as in 1 above, but the girl nevertheless changes her attitude to the man as a result of his words, saying to herself, perhaps, something like: 'Well, I never realised he was the kind of person who appreciated a beautiful sunset!'
3. It may be *a genuine communication situation,* i.e. part at least of the man's motive in saying these words is to change the girl's attitude towards him.
4. The words are used by the man as *a way of striking up acquaintance* with the girl; he is using his remark as a way of opening up a channel of communication between them.

For discussion
Which of the following would you consider communication situations? For those in which you think communication is taking place indicate:

1. who is the Tx, who the Rx,
2. what feedback there is, if any,
3. how successfully communication is taking place.

(*a*) You are watching a cricket match and the batsman makes a fine cover drive to the boundary. 'Good shot!' says the man in the seat in front of you.
(*b*) Your name is Joe. Jack is stacking away groceries. When he gets to two big crates of canned fruit he calls out: 'Hey Joe! Give me a hand a minute; these crates are more than I can manage on my own.'
(*c*) A drunk lurches up to you when you are in a bus queue and says. 'Is this where you get the bus for Higglewick?' (There is such a place and although he has a job getting his lips round the name you can just recognise it.)
(*d*) A drunk lurches up to you in a bus queue and says: 'Lot of bleeders, they are. Rotten stinking swine. What they want to do a thing like

that for? To me of all people. When did I ever do anything to them, eh? I ask you. When did I ever do anything to them? Rotten bleeders.' He lurches away again.

(e) Two mums are talking, Mrs Brown and Mrs Green.

Mrs Brown: My Alison's never been the same since she started going to the Tech.

Mrs Green: My Tim's changed a lot too since he's been going there.

Mrs Brown: Quiet little thing she always was. Now it's buy, buy, all the time. Everything for her own back. Costs me something, I can tell you.

Mrs Green: He wouldn't do any work at school, you know. Never would do a thing. Now he stays in every night doing his homework.

Mrs Brown: Out every night she is. Always off to some hop or other, or a disco. Comes in all hours too.

Mrs Green: He's taking his examinations at the end of this year and then he'll have a proper qualification, which is more than his father ever had.

Mrs Brown: I don't know how she'll end up. Proper worry to me she is that girl. And only since she's being going to that place . . .

(f) *Customer*: Can you tell me if this curtain material is fade-proof?

Assistant: That's Trinalon, Madam. One of the hardest wearing curtain materials there is. Very opaque too – keeps out the light better than velvet. We've never had any complaints about it.

(g) You have been away on a week's course. On the first day back the boss passes you in a corridor. 'Ah. So you're back again,' he says, as he walks by.

(h) *Manager*: Listen. We've put the price of our special sausages up 3p but we've improved them as well. They've got 5 per cent more meat in them now and they're in a new type of casing. We've changed the seasoning a bit too.

Assistant: What's the point of the new casings, if anybody asks?

Manager: Well they're artificial and some people don't like the sound of that, so you had better be careful how you talk about them. But they're a lot easier to get your teeth through than the old natural skins.

(i) *Customer*: The sausages have gone up a lot this week.

Assistant: Yes, madam, but we've improved the quality.

Customer: That's what they always say when they put the price of anything up.

Assistant: Well, madam, it's true this time. They are tastier, crisper to bite through and they've got 5 per cent more meat in them. You try them.

(j) *Customer*: Have these sausages got plastic skins?

Assistant (*not the same one as in the previous example!*): Yes.

IV. Basic communication principles

The fundamental principle of good communication is that when you are the Tx you think in terms of your Rx. You try to see everything from his point of view. You do not therefore baffle him by pouring out all you know on the subject; you pick out the information he needs to know if he is to make the response you want. You do not choose words to show what a big vocabulary you have: you choose words that you think the Rx will understand.

You do not think in terms of your Rx because you are unselfish; you do so because you have a purpose in communicating – you want a certain response from him. You must therefore do everything you can to make it easy for the Rx to understand you, and this means adjusting your message to suit the individual Rx. Take, as an example, the sales assistant selling tape recorders. He could not use the same approach for a rather silly young woman who hardly seemed to know what a tape recorder was as he had just used with a well-educated prosperous middle-aged man whose first questions revealed that he was a Hi-Fi enthusiast.

Know your Rx is a basic rule of good communication.

The sort of thing it is desirable to know if you are going to communicate effectively includes:

1. the sex of the Rx
2. his/her age (approximately, and particularly in relation to yours)
3. his/her apparent intelligence level
4. his/her apparent social/financial standing
5. his/her apparent educational level
6. his/her previous knowledge of the matter which is the subject of communication.

A most important part of communication therefore consists in picking up all the clues we can that will give us this kind of information about our Rx and thus help us to plan what we say or write to suit him/her. This is not too difficult when we have the Rx in front of us in shop, salon, or restaurant. We can get valuable information about the Rx by unobtrusively noting such points as facial expression; bearing; the sort of clothes he/she is wearing (not merely how new, or how expensive); hair style; tone of voice; accent. It is much more difficult when we are talking over the telephone, and very difficult indeed when we have perhaps only a single letter from the customer to get to know him/her by.

For discussion
1. What points other than those mentioned already might give you clues about an Rx who is talking to you?
2. What clues might you obtain over the telephone?
3. What clues might you obtain from a letter?

The all-important preliminary study of the Rx fits into a communication sequence that you should follow whenever you have to communicate to anybody at any length. The stages are as follows:

1. *Define your purpose.* We always communicate for a reason. What is yours? What response(s) are you aiming at? We nearly always have more than one response in mind. For example, our chief aim may be *Rx buys the product* but we will also want the Rx to develop a favourable attitude

towards us. We want him to think us helpful, just, knowledgeable, efficient, friendly etc. This matter of attitude is particularly important in such jobs as hairdressing and waiting.

2. *Prepare your information.* Make sure you have sufficient information. Get your ideas clear in your head. Get your ideas in order.

3. *Study your* Rx.

4. *Select your information.* Now you know something about your Rx you can pick out what parts of your information the Rx *must* know. What is relevant to the response you require? What is the minimum you can tell him and yet communicate effectively?

5. *Adapt your medium to your* Rx. For example, if your Rx seems unintelligent and ill-educated you may have to simplify your vocabulary, avoid technical words, use short sentences, speak slowly.

6. *Provide for feedback.* Make it easy for the Rx to give you feedback. If you are writing, for example, encourage the Rx to write, phone, call at the showroom, etc. if he wants further information.

7. *Act on feedback.* Do not ignore feedback. If you are speaking, alter the way you are transmitting your message if the Rx shows the slightest misunderstanding or opposition.

Group activity

Each member of the group imagines himself in a typical communication situation to do with his work. He is to invent details; for example, in retailing, what article he is selling and what sort of customer he is dealing with. He describes the situation to the group and shows how the seven communication stages apply. Each contribution is followed by group discussion.

V. Communication and retailing

In this section the generalisations about communication outlined in the preceding sections are applied to retailing, with special reference to large stores. Students from other trades, or from smaller retailers, will be able to make their own adjustment of this material to suit their particular circumstances.

To begin with, the sales assistant will be involved with the internal communication system of his store. He will be an Rx when receiving instructions from his departmental manager, a Tx when reporting damaged goods or a customer complaint. He will have to read leaflets and other communication material supplied by manufacturers so that he knows all he can about his stock. He will have to familiarise himself with standard instructions relating to such matters as timekeeping, dress, cashing-up routines, making out receipts, and procedure in accepting cheques.

By far the most important use he will make of communications is, however, in dealing with customers. An important application of his communication skill will be ensuring that the customer finds his visit to the store pleasant and – even if he does not buy anything in that department – leaves feeling that the store as a whole, and that department in particular, is polite, helpful, knowledgeable.

Occasionally he will have to deal with quite demanding communication situations, for example a complaint. In dealing with a complaint his first consideration is to decide whether it is justified or not. If it *is* justified he will: (1) have to decide (or ask his departmental manager to decide) what adjustments can be made that will satisfy the customer without too much loss to the firm; (2) explain what has happened and apologise in such a way that the customer's dissatisfaction with the store is reduced; (3) send the customer away feeling that, despite this mistake, the store is a good one and worthy of his continued custom. If the complaint is *not* justified the demands on the assistant's communication skill is probably greater. He may have to point out that the fault lies with the customer, not the store, and do this without antagonising him or making him feel a fool. He may decide that the customer was being unreasonable, even dishonest, in complaining. In such circumstances it is a tricky communication feat to make it clear to the customer that his attempt to get away with it has been seen through, yet not antagonise him to such a degree that he goes round trying to get his own back by continuous propaganda against the store.

In such situations particularly heavy demands are made on the assistant's judgment, tact, charm and – above all – skill in using words. These communication qualities are, in fact, required in most of the assistant's contacts with customers, including all but the simplest and most routine of sales.

Selling is always a communication situation. If the customer knows exactly what he wants and the store has it in stock, the communication demand on the assistant is slight. His contribution may be no more than one of accepting the money, wrapping up the item, and giving a pleasant smile. If real selling is involved (i.e. the assistant has to work to make a sale) the full communication process is in operation. Figure 3 represents

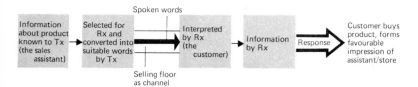

Figure 3.

diagrammatically the communication activity involved in completing a successful sale. It is highly simplified, of course, because it does not take into consideration feedback, or the times when the customer becomes the Tx and the assistant the Rx. The course of a difficult sale is bound, in practice, to be a dialogue situation.

3
Speaking and Writing

I. Differences between speech and writing: Words

It is a mistake to think that writing is simply speech written down. That is the way writing started, of course, but once a written form of language has been established it is very slow to change. Oral language, on the other hand, is changing all the time – people are always thinking up new ways of saying what they want to say – or using old words in new senses to fit new circumstances. The spoken language and the written language quickly get out of step with each other and at any particular moment of history there is bound to be a great deal of difference between the way people write and the way they speak. This does not mean that what people say that is different from the written language is wrong – it is just different.

Gradually many of the new words (or old words in new senses) that have been developed in the spoken language become absorbed into the written language. At the time this book was written this could be seen happening with words such as *hippy, junkie, gear* (clothes and accessories). They were just coming out of the stage of being used only in speech and beginning to appear in writing – first in rather informal writing, as in newspapers and magazines, then, more slowly, in books. They were still not so fully accepted as to be suitable for completely formal writing such as a report or a business letter and will probably still not be by the time you are reading this.

Words and expressions which are current in speech but not fully accepted into the written language are called 'colloquialisms'. The various stages of acceptance into writing of a colloquialism can be seen by looking at an up-to-date dictionary. While the word is still only suitable for speech it does not appear at all (except in special dictionaries of slang and colloquialisms). There is then a transitional phase when it appears in dictionaries but is followed by the abbreviation *col* or *coll*. Finally when it is fully accepted and can be used in even the most formal writing it is entered like any other word.

The word *trip* is a typical example of what we are discussing. In the sense of a little jump or falling over something it is a very ancient part of the written language. In the sense of a visit it was still considered colloquial at the beginning of the nineteenth century although now, of course, fully accepted in all types of writing. In the sense of a drug-induced fantasy it is at the time of writing considered colloquial, but acceptable in some forms of writing. It cannot, however, be used in this sense in formal writing – a medical report for example.

Not all colloquialisms become incorporated into the written language with the passing of time. Many simply die out. Others stay colloquial – for example *alright,* which has existed since the eighteenth century but is still not considered suitable for the more formal kinds of writing (e.g. business letters, official announcements, legal documents, reports – and examination answers).

Most colloquialisms are acceptable in speech in all circumstances, although there is a tendency in very formal circumstances (an interview for a job, for example) to keep use of them to a minimum. They can, of course, be used in writing if the writing is imitating speech, as in dialogue in a novel or a play, or in personal letters when we want to sound as if we are talking to our friends, not writing.

One category of colloquialism, slang, cannot be used in all circumstances. 'Slang' is a matter of deliberately substituting an undignified word for the more widely approved equivalent – for example *nosh* for 'food', or *a right Charley* for 'a silly fellow'. Slang, because it is undignified, is not general suitable for use outside the circle of friends and relatives (and not all the latter will accept it!) It is not suitable for use with customers (unless you know them very well and think they will appreciate your introduction of a little slang into what you say).

A good deal of slang is 'obscene' in that it makes open or hidden reference to excretion, or sex, or the parts of the body concerned in these human activities (which also figure largely in swearing.) Everybody realises that such slang must be avoided in talking to customers. As discussion of it (especially in mixed classes) also causes embarrassment to many, obscene slang is therefore omitted from consideration here apart from this reference.

When a colloquialism is first introduced into writing it is sometimes put between inverted commas as if it were an unfamiliar technical word. Thus when *gear* was new in that sense (early 1960s) a fashion writer might have written *Young people today are increasingly turning to Carnaby Street for their 'gear'.* The inverted commas here mean 'as they call it'. This stage lasts a very short time. It is not necessary to place all words that have recently been colloquialisms between inverted commas – and putting inverted commas round a colloquialism not acceptable in writing does not make it acceptable.

You will see that when we write something down instead of saying it we have a special problem: perhaps some of the words we would have used in saying it are not available to us in writing. We have to know, roughly at least, which of the words we use in our daily speech are considered colloquial if our writing is not to seem too much like speech written down. We also need to decide which of the colloquialisms we employ are a little too slangy for use in our work even in speech (and this is a very difficult decision to make).

The opposite also applies to some extent. Some of the words we pick up from books seem to other people too formal or too long for use in everyday speech. If we use them (although it may be correct to use them) we sound pompous, conceited, or old-fashioned, perhaps, to others. 'He talks like a book' is not really a complimentary thing to say of somebody.

To sum up, people who are inclined to be bookworms sometimes find it difficult to speak in a simple natural way that everybody will accept. On the other hand people who have done most of their communicating by means of the oral language (and this will mean almost everybody using this book) often have difficulty in finding the right words to use when they have to put something down in writing.

For discussion

The forty words and phrases below are all ones which are – or have been – considered colloquial. They constitute a tiny percentage of the many thousands of such expressions that people have some doubt about using in their jobs. Discussion of this small selection is intended to help you in making up your mind about all such expressions.

Try to put each into one of the following categories:

1. Slangy – not suitable for use with customers.
2. Colloquial – acceptable when speaking to customers but not to be used in writing.
3. Colloquial – beginning to appear in informal writing (newspapers, magazines, advertising etc) but not suitable for formal writing.
4. No longer colloquial – acceptable in all forms of writing including business letters and examination answers.

You will find this quite difficult and there will probably be some disagreement between members of the group. This is partly because the categories oversimplify. In practice there are a huge number of such categories – for example: slang suitable for your friends may not be suitable with your family; some customers will not mind – might even prefer – a certain amount of slang in what you say; some business letters can be made more human by one or two colloquialisms of a sort that would normally be considered acceptable only in private letters, and so on. A further cause of argument is that the situation over colloquialisms and slang is changing all the time and it is difficult to be completely up-to-date.

NOTE. Many of these words and phrases have more than one meaning, some of which may never have been considered colloquial. For such expressions it is only the meaning indicated in brackets that is to be discussed.

grotty; *conk*; *dud*; *lousy* (of poor quality); *spot on*; *sleazy*; *a write-off*; *a facer* (sudden obstacle); *hankie*; *hard put to it*; *to fall over backwards* (try almost too hard); *fake* (a sham); *to pack in* (to stop working, of machine or person); *to muscle in*; *bent* (criminal); *dodgy* (difficult, likely to go wrong); *racket* (line of business, as *What racket are you in?*); *the rag trade* (the garments industry); *fair enough*; *bind* (nuisance); *on the never-never*; *funny* (strange, odd); *corny* (old-fashioned, sentimental); *ropey*; *dead dozy*; *on the ball* (opposite to *dead dozy*); *cool* (very satisfactory or attractive); *beat-up* (old and well used); *off-beat*; *trendy*; *kooky*; *drag* (something boring); *drag* (female costume worn by men); *spiel* (an explanation or sales talk); *nick* (steal); *way out* (in advance of fashion); *flake out* (to faint); *hard up* (not having much money); *broke* (without money); *skint* (without money).

II. Differences between speech and writing: Grammar

You will be pleased to learn that you will not be hearing very much about 'grammar' in this book; the idea is to help you communicate in both speech and writing, not to teach you grammar. But it is worth noting that many grammatical points that careful writers concern themselves with are treated differently in speech. For example it is correct to write: *It is important to establish to whom this account was addressed. Who* in this sentence would not do. A spoken version of this sentence would be something like: *We must know who this account was addressed to.* The first of these two sentences would still be possible if spoken – but it would sound stiff and unnatural to most people. The second sentence would not be acceptable in writing – chiefly because of the *who*, but the whole sentence has the characteristic ring of speech rather than writing.

Here is another example of this kind of difference of attitude towards minor grammatical points. In speech somebody might say, perfectly acceptably: *Do you mind me checking over the figures myself?* If he wrote this (and was a careful and experienced writer) he would probably put: *Do you mind my checking over the figures myself?* (because what might be minded is not the writer – *me* – but the checking).

More important – although in writing we are supposed to use complete sentences (there is a great deal about this to come, in Chapter 7) in speech we often use incomplete ones. Thus we can say: *Just going to check the reserve stock out the back. Won't be a minute.* The written version of this would be *I am just going to check the reserve stock out the back. I won't be a minute.* (i.e. it would have to be in complete sentences). In fact there would probably be more changes than that because a careful and experienced writer would very likely decide that *out the back* and *won't* were a little too colloquial (unless the message was for his mate, not the boss). In practice he would probably – for the boss – write something like: *I have just gone to check the reserve stock in the store at the back of the unloading area. I shall not be away long.*

Are you beginning to get some idea of the kind of difference there is between speaking and writing? Perhaps this would be a good time to discuss this in class.

For discussion
What kinds of difference are there between the spoken and written versions of messages? Does it matter to whom the message is being transmitted (i.e. can this make the difference greater or smaller?)

III. Pronunciation

In the preceding section we tried to think a little about the differences in phrasing between speech and writing. It is one of the major problems of a novelist, playwright, or TV writer. The novelist (some of the time) and the other two (all the time) have to make what they *write* sound like people *speaking*.

Here are a few lines of dialogue after something has been stolen from a store. First as written by a writer with no ear at all for the way people really speak – it sounds like writing, not speech:

> DEPARTMENTAL MANAGER: *What did the person who stole this item look like?*
> ASSISTANT: *He was a tall old gentleman wearing gold-rimmed spectacles.*

Here is a much better version that in a novel or play would pass at pretty convincing speech:

> DEPARTMENTAL MANAGER: *What did he look like, the one who took it?*
> ASSISTANT: *Tall old fellow with gold-rimmed glasses.*

This is about as far as most writers go in trying to sound convincing. It is still not very much like the real thing. Unless the departmental manager and assistant were exceptionally careful speakers their actual pronunciation of these words would be slurred and abbreviated – much more difficult for the ear to distinguish than the words as written above would be if, for example, read out by a BBC newsreader.

Exactly how they would speak the words would vary a little according to the part of the country they came from (although this slurring is not a dialect matter) but supposing both were from the south-east the dialogue might seem a little more convincing written like this:

> DEPARTMENTAL MANAGER: *Wodidee look like, the wunoo tookit?*
> ASSISTANT: *Tallole feller wi goalrim glasses.*

For discussion
Here are a few more attempts at reproducing what people really say (and it is, of course, customers as well as assistants who speak like this, including those who are well educated and would consider themselves upper class). If what you have heard people saying locally seems a little different try to write out – as a group activity – local versions. Remember, though, it is slurring, not dialect, we are thinking about principally.

> This is strickly private – juss between Ewenme.
> Shove over thack crater corm beef.
> Gimme a cuppla tim peaches willya?
> People like what they're useter. Frinstance mose people like bacononeggs.

Compare these with versions closer to the written form. Which version is easier to understand? Which sounds more pleasing? Do you think it matters if people speak rather like these examples?

Although some of the previous examples would seem to suggest that greater clarity results from pronouncing words more carefully it is not true that to speak correctly we have to pronounce words as they are spelled. The word *spelled* itself is always pronounced *spelt* (and can be spelled that way too); we do not attempt to pronounce the *b* in *subtle*. People who speak much more than they read and write become nervous about differences between spelling and pronunciation and sometimes unnecessarily alter their pronunciation to fit the spelling. But spelling has remained unchanged for centuries while pronunciation alters over the years – so spelling may not be at all a sound guide to pronunciation.

In the past there was a tendency for the children of unskilled working class parents to lack confidence in the way they and their parents said words and to try to 'correct' the family pronunciation by pronouncing every word exactly as it was spelled. This resulted in a curious kind of class distinction in the way certain words were pronounced. Differences of this kind, between working-class and middle-class pronunciation, can still be detected today, the working class version being invariably the one closer to the spelling.

For discussion

1. What about the pronunciation of the following words?

   forehead, Holborn, clerk, Derby, medicine, waistcoat, advertisement, chaos, tortoise, template.

2. You can hear the word 'extraordinary' pronounced four ways – as six, five, four or three syllables. Which do you prefer?

IV. Non-verbal factors in oral communication

There is much more to oral communication than the words we use. In writing, the words are all the medium we have.

Consider the waiter who says to a customer: *The duck's orf.* A waiter who prided himself on doing his job well would say something like: *I'm very sorry, Sir. We've had quite a run on the duck and there's no more left. But the chicken's very good – real farm chickens, not frozen ones. I can recommend the chicken.* The second waiter has chosen much more helpful things to say and picked his words carefully to seem tactful and sympathetic to a disappointed customer. (It is assumed that what he says is *true*.) But in such a case it would not be only the two waiters' *words* that would be communicating to the customer. The first waiter would (almost certainly) also communicate by his manner, facial expression, tone of voice etc., his ill-concealed satisfaction at disappointing a customer. The second waiter would, by the same additional media, undoubtedly communicate his genuine regret at not being able to give the customer exactly what he wanted and his intention to be helpful.

When we speak, other media operate in parallel to the main medium of words. These media include such factors as volume and tone of voice, facial expression, gestures. Less obvious points are also involved such as how we stand (think of yourself in front of the boss's desk), how we dress, even what sort of hair style we have or, if males, how much unshaved hair there is on our faces. These all say something about our attitude (to our work, to the customer, to life outside work etc.) and a little of this is communicated to the Rx. Most of this communication is, for the majority of people, of the unconscious kind that we looked at in Chapter 2. If you want to improve your oral communication with customers you have to become much more aware of these parallel media than the average person is.

Waiters, sales assistants, hairdressers etc. have to be to some extent actors. They have to learn to control facial expression and tone of voice, for example, so that these line up with what is being said and support it. A sales assistant who says: *I'm sorry, Madam* has to look and sound sorry as well as speaking the words. They have also to give some consideration to such points as: whether what they wear is appropriate to their work; whether the way they stand makes them seem enthusiastic and alert or couldn't-care-less; whether they smile or look surly when they greet a customer; whether they are successfully disguising at all times boredom, weariness, a headache, irritation with a troublesome customer etc., or whether their facial expression and tone of voice are giving them away.

For discussion
From the point of view of non-verbal communication consider the following:

(*a*) With reference to your own work (*b*) in terms of the conclusions you would draw if you were the customer.

1. The three assistants in the store who go on chatting to each other although a customer is waiting.
2. The girl assistant who a few minutes after the store has opened is combing her hair.
3. The importance of the appearance of hands for sales assistants, hairdressers, waiters and waitresses.
4. Whether a male assistant is wearing a tie or not. What sort of tie he is wearing.
5. The importance of a smile.
6. What sort of impression is given at work by shoes – for example (males): well-polished black; suede, dark brown; suede, light fawn; dirty black; plimsolls.
7. What advantages are gained by having all asssistants similarly dressed? What sort of dress would seem appropriate? Are there any disadvantages in similarity?
8. How much does a smart appearance and good grooming matter?
9. How can an assistant seem friendly and helpful apart from what he/she says?
10. When the assistant says: 'I am very sorry, Madam but . . .' is he/she usually sorry? Does the customer usually know whether he is or not? How much does tone of voice affect what we say?

4
Putting Your Ideas in Order

I. Words are linear

Words are the most accurate and flexible method of communication that we have at our command but they have one serious disadvantage. Words are linear – that is to say the Tx has to use them one after each other as if in a line. It therefore takes time for the Rx to find out what the Tx is telling him. This is particularly difficult in oral communication when the Rx can only guess what the next word is going to be and has to wait patiently as the Tx adds word to word to make up his message. At least in reading he can glance ahead to get an idea of what is coming (and quick readers always do this).

There is no way with words to give the Rx all the information at once (as we can with a picture, a graph, a table of statistics) and let him decide for himself in what order to take it in. The Tx is in control of what he is going to tell the Rx first, what second. The Tx has the job of breaking up what he is going to say or write into pieces and he decides the order of those pieces. We all make such decisions every time we speak or write. The unfortunate Rx has to accept what we do; he cannot change the way we have divided up the material or the order in which we have put it. It is up to us therefore (when we are the Tx) to divide up our material logically and to put it into an order that will be helpful to the Rx. If we do not think about this the Rx will become terribly confused as we jump about from point to point and will find it very difficult to follow what we are telling him.

The whole art of putting our ideas in order for transmission by words consists therefore in:

1. dividing the material into logical sections.
2. deciding the best order in which to present the sections to the Rx.

These logical sections are not very apparent when we are speaking (although they are certainly there if we have thought out what we are going to say properly). In writing they are quite clear, becoming the paragraphs of a letter, an article, an examination answer; the chapters of a book; the various numbered divisions and subdivisions of a report or well-arranged notes.

Putting our ideas in order before transmission is essential to successful oral and written communication. You will find that during this course we shall keep returning to the basic methods of doing so described in this chapter. It is not very easy material to meet so early on – but because it is fundamental it must be tackled quickly, and mastered.

II. Logical sections

We break up what we have to communicate so that it can be transmitted to the Rx piece by piece in a logical way by one of two methods – by analysis or by classification.

ANALYSIS

We may have a rather complicated whole that we break down into the various parts from which it is made up. This is called 'analysis'. Each part in our analysis should seem complete in itself and clearly separate from all the others. It is rather like a butcher dividing up a carcase. He does not just chop it into horrible looking cubes of about the size he thinks best. He looks for the joints of the bones and divides the meat into anatomical sections – shoulder, leg, rump etc – that are recognisable divisions of the whole beast. Similarly, in describing an appliance we divide it into its component parts, a process into its various stages. The chapters of this book were arrived at after a process of analysis.

CLASSIFICATION

Our organisational problem may, on the other hand, be that we have a large number of small points to make that would be very confusing if transmitted to the Rx just as we happened to think of them. In such a case we have to think of ways that we can rearrange these points in a comparatively small number of groups that will be easier to control. All the points in any one group have to have something in common that permits us to put them together. This progress is called 'classification'. We look through our list of points and put each one into a class. Then all the points in the same class are gathered together and dealt with in one section of our communication.

Analysis and classification are fundamental processes in all organisation, and have much wider application than in communication alone. Anything we have to organise we control by one or both of these methods.

The organisation of a large store is a convenient example. If we are considering the total work of the store we find it much easier to examine if we first break it down into separate kinds of work – for example: buying; selling; delivery; advertising; administration etc. In other words, we analyse the work carried out. If, on the other hand, we try to think of all the many thousands of separate types of item sold in the store our minds cannot control such varied information unless we can group the items that belong together. We group them into such sections as: women's wear; men's wear; kitchen goods; hardware; furniture; soft furnishings. In other words, we use classification to provide order and system. You will

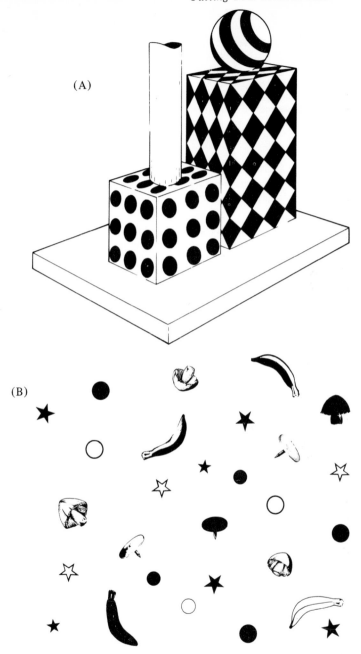

Figure 4.

see immediately that classification is in fact the organisational basis of all departmental stores.

Similarly, it would be very confusing for customers in a supermarket if all the items on sale were placed on the shelves wherever the manager felt like it – so that mixed pickles were next to custard powder and pickled onions were right the other side of the shop between soups and biscuits. The manager has to give thought to this, and see that similar types of item are next to each other on the shelves. To do this he has to put every item on sale into a class as, for example, tinned meats; tinned fish; soups; jams; pickles; biscuits (sweet); biscuits (for cheese) etc.

For discussion

A. Figure 4 looks very puzzling. (A) and (B) represent material which is suitable either for classification or for analysis.

1. Which is which?
2. How would you carry out the classification/analysis involved?
3. Try to put the two groups of logical sections you have arrived at in a logical order. Can you agree amongst yourselves?
4. If so, can you explain why you chose that particular order for each?

B. How would you analyse the following items if you had to write a description of them?

1. a tennis racquet
2. a technical college
3. your classroom
4. the contents of a newspaper
5. your working day

C. How would you analyse into stages?

1. the process of making a sale
2. ordering a meal in a restaurant
3. doing a 'perm' *or* starting a car
4. enrolling at a technical college
5. joining a public library

D. Suggest several methods by which you could classify each of the following and consider their advantages and disadvantages:

1. a mixed collection of records
2. students at your college
3. all the books you own
4. magazines
5. items on a shopping list.

(You will soon discover that the advantages and disadvantages of different methods of classification cannot be discussed properly until you have agreed upon why you are making the classification.)

E. How would you organise the Coats section of the Women's Wear department of a large London departmental store with a well-off middle-class clientele?

F. How would you organise a few rails of coats in a small women's wear shop sited in a working-class area of a large provincial town?

III. Logical order

For discussion
A. Arrange the following in logical order (*not* alphabetical order)

1. winter, spring, autumn, summer
2. March, February, December, June, August, May
3. London, Swindon, Bath, Reading, Weston-super-Mare, Bristol
4. (Customers' income and job categories): middle class; upper working class; the poorest; upper middle class; lower middle class
5. (Advertising media): magazines; newspapers; television; posters; cinema
6. The departments of your college
7. Cricket, football (association), football (rugby), lacrosse, hockey, polo.

B. On what principle did you arrange each group in order?

Putting what we have to tell the Rx into a logical order that will help him to understand us is not easy. You were banned from using alphabetical order in the discussion work because alphabetical order (although very useful for looking things up) is not helpful to the Rx. You would not make much sense of a lesson in which the teacher dealt with everything in alphabetical order – you expect the teacher to choose an order that takes you step-by-step through what you have to learn, each point preparing the way for what follows. That is what we really need in every communication situation. Sometimes material falls readily into a natural order and we hardly have to think about it; more often it is essential to sort out what we have to say before we start and decide on some principle by which we are going to put it into order.

A. Some sort of INTRODUCTION is usually necessary. If you start immediately on the facts before the Rx knows what you are talking, or writing, about he will find it very difficult to grasp the first part of what you are telling him. He needs to be prepared for what is to come. In oral communication we use a lead-in such as: *You know those Danish teasets you were asking about last week? Well, I've found out a bit more about them.* In writing, a title or heading is often sufficient (in this book, for example, each chapter and each section has a title for this purpose). Sometimes an introductory sentence is necessary, or in longer work a whole paragraph, to establish the WHAT, WHO, WHERE, WHEN of what is to follow (i.e. what are we going to be told about? – who did it? – where and when did it take place?). We do not, of course, always need to introduce all these points – the 'what' alone is often enough.

B. Some sort of CONCLUSION is needed at the end of a piece of communication unless it is very short and simple. In writing, this may just round off the description or letter neatly; with fairly complicated material it may summarise what has gone before. In speech, we often repeat what we have been saying in a shortened form as the conclusion (since the Rx has no other way of receiving the information a second time – with writing, of course, he can reread as often as he needs to), or remind our Rx briefly of what we want him to do.

C. Between introduction and conclusion lies the MAIN BODY of the information we are transmitting. The following are the methods most commonly used for arranging the main body in a helpful order if the material does not immediately fall into an obvious natural order.

1. CHRONOLOGICAL ORDER. Suitable for describing action. Events are described in the order in which they took place.

2. SPATIAL ORDER. Facts are given on a geographical basis (north to south, progressively outward from London etc.) or goods, buildings, etc. described left to right, front to back etc.)

3. ASCENDING ORDER OF IMPORTANCE. Mostly used in literary work. To keep the Rx reading (or listening) the most interesting or exciting sections of the material are held back to the end. Not very often used at work – the customer may walk away if you do not bring out the big selling points quickly; the boss may not read your report at all if you spend a lot of time at the beginning on minor points. Arguments are, however, usually best presented in this way, building up your case with more and more powerful reasons and bringing out your strongest point of all at the end when the Rx is already half convinced.

4. DESCENDING ORDER OF IMPORTANCE. It follows from what was said about ascending order that its opposite is the approved method for selling and report-writing. A very useful method for all business communication. The most important point is made while the Rx's attention is at maximum; minor matters are left to the end.

5. ASCENDING ORDER OF COMPLEXITY. The simplest part of the material is put first so that the Rx is not discouraged by being plumped straight into something complicated, or difficult to understand. When he has grasped the simpler points you can gradually introduce the more difficult ones. This is the teacher's method – but it is also very useful with customers, especially when technical information is involved. If, for example, you are selling a rather complicated appliance, you want to make it seem simple at first, otherwise you may frighten your potential purchaser away.

6. ASCENDING ORDER OF FAMILIARITY. Another teaching method which is valuable with customers. You start with what the Rx knows about already, and only gradually introduce what will probably be new to him. Very useful when *explaining* (how an appliance works, for example).

For discussion

A. The six methods of placing material in logical order that you have just been studying had themselves to be placed in logical order by the author. On what basis do you think he decided on the order employed?

B. The person who wrote the following seems not to have given sufficient thought to putting his sentences in a logical order that would help to make the process described clear to the Rx. How can the order be improved? The sentences are lettered for convenient reference in discussion.

(*a*) The loaves go in at the top of the machine and are carried by two moving belts down to the blades.

(*b*) As each loaf is pushed against them it is cut into slices and pushed out through the blades onto the end of a reel of waxed paper.

(*c*) The blades are very sharp, fixed upright in rows, and kept jogging up and down in a sawing motion by an electric motor.

(*d*) Next, two arms come from the sides of the machine and fold the paper over the ends of the loaf.

(*e*) Although bread has been on sale for hundreds of years in shops, it is only in recent years that people have been able to buy it ready cut into slices and wrapped in waxed paper.

(*f*) The paper is automatically pulled up and over the loaf and adjusted to the right size before being sheared off.

(*g*) The whole wrapped loaf is then pushed between electrically heated pressure plates.

(*h*) The heat of these melts the wax on the surface of the paper so that it acts like glue holding the folds in position.

(*i*) Although it would take a long time to cut the loaves up and wrap them by hand, an automatic electric slicer and wrapper makes very short work of it.

C. Similarly, decide by discussion the most satisfactory order for the items in the following fireworks safety code.

(*a*) Light fireworks at arm's length – preferably with a safety firework lighter or fuse wick.

(*b*) Never fool with fireworks.

(*c*) Never put fireworks in your pocket.

(*d*) Follow the instructions on each firework carefully; read them by torchlight – never a naked flame.

(*e*) Keep fireworks in a closed box; take them out one at a time and put the lid back at once.

(*f*) Never throw fireworks.

(*g*) Never return to a firework once lit – it may go off in your face.

(*h*) Stand well back.

(*i*) Keep pets indoors.

Exercise 1

The instructions that follow have been printed in a confused order. By rearranging the sentences in a logical order you can produce the recipe for a rather unusual dish – Carelien Stew. The most unusual feature of this is that it includes more than one kind of meat. In France (where it originated) it is usually prepared with equal quantities of stewing steak, pork, lamb, and veal.

Serve the meat surrounded by the potatoes and vegetables.

Quantities are for four people.

Cut the meat into cubes and slice the onions and carrots.

For this dish you will require one pound of lean meat of at least two different kinds, two onions, two carrots, and a pound of potatoes.

Peel and quarter the potatoes.

Put the meat, onions, and carrots into a saucepan and cover with water. The liquid in which the meat and vegetables have been cooked makes a good basis for soup.

Add the potatoes, with salt and pepper to taste, and continue cooking for 20 minutes.

Bring to the boil and simmer for 40 minutes.

5
Speaking to Communicate

I. Speaking clearly

Speaking to communicate is above all a matter of speaking clearly. Of course, as with all forms of communication, *what* you have to communicate is very important – but if you do not speak clearly you may not succeed in communicating anything at all.

If we think about it for a moment we shall see that when we say 'speaking clearly' we are talking about two different things at the same time. We mean both (1) making the sounds of speech sufficiently loudly and distinctly that the listener can have no doubt at all what words we are saying, and (2) choosing words that convey our message without distortion, and putting what we have to say in a logical order so that it is easy for the Rx to follow what we are telling him. The second of these is a standard communication aim but it is particularly difficult to achieve in speech because we have very little time to think ahead – we usually have to pick our words and put our ideas in order *while we are speaking*.

We have just looked at putting our ideas in order – and a great deal of this book is about putting our ideas into words. In this section therefore we shall look chiefly at the first meaning of 'speaking clearly'.

Making the sounds of speech loudly enough for the situation we find ourselves in (*audibility*) is simply a matter of pushing sufficient air through our vocal chords. We learn by experience the kind of adjustment we need to make between, say, talking across the breakfast table and talking across a sales counter. If there is a greater distance between us and our Rx than we are accustomed to we realise we have to push through more air and increase our volume. If there is background noise we again need more volume, to overcome the competition for the listener's ear. A room with poor acoustics also requires a special vocal effort from us.

Our judgment in these matters improves as we get older. Many young people, because of their lack of experience, underestimate the volume required, especially in formal circumstances such as in the classroom or at work, and are therefore very difficult to hear.

A further factor producing a poor standard of audibility in girls and young men of the age of the expected readers of this book is shyness, selfconsciousness, a reluctance to draw attention to themselves by speaking out. It is noticeable that young people usually employ plenty of vocal energy when chatting to each other; it is when they talk to somebody considerably older than themselves or find themselves in a fairly formal speech situation (such as answering a question in class, advising a customer, reporting to the boss) that their voices suddenly fall away to an almost inaudible mumble.

It is worth while struggling to overcome inaudibility, and your classes in communication provide a very convenient opportunity. Take an active part in all class discussion, and also involve yourself in any debates organised by your college. If possible, try to obtain committee experience with your Students' Union as well.

It may help you to overcome inaudibility to remember that your own voice always sounds much louder to you than it does to others. It may also help to take a deep breath or two before you start to speak. But the biggest change will come when you stop thinking about yourself and instead start thinking about: (1) your Rx, (2) what you want to tell him, (3) what you want him to do as a result of what you say.

Volume alone is not enough to ensure clear speech. The sounds you make must be carefully and accurately produced so that the Rx has no difficulty in distinguishing one sound from another. This is called 'articulation'. It is largely a matter of lips, jaw, tongue, teeth. It is difficult to distinguish what is said by somebody who has a hare lip; or badly fitting false teeth; or who has just lost a tooth, and gained a split lip, as the result of an argument. Similarly if you move your lips, jaw, tongue clumsily or carelessly, or do not place your tongue accurately in relation to your teeth in words like *top, this, thistle,* your listener will find it difficult to distinguish what you are saying. The more exactly and quickly you can move the organs of articulation the clearer your voice will be.

Again shyness and self-consciousness come into it. Young people sometimes feel that they must look rather ridiculous opening their mouths wide, shifting their tongues round, moving their lips about (for words like *temporary* or *geography*), dropping their jaws down (for words like *jaw*) etc. They do not look ridiculous, of course, as everybody has to make such mouth movements to speak successfully – they will certainly *sound* ridiculous if they try to talk without moving their mouths. Talking without moving the mouth should be left to ventriloquists. (If you talk without opening your mouth sufficiently, by the way, most of your voice comes out through your nose – it is then not very loud and sounds extremely odd.)

Sometimes people who are really trying to articulate distinctly seem to concentrate on the beginnings of words and lose the endings. When they do this it is difficult to decide if they are saying 'That will be fifty p' or 'That will be fifteen p'. Similarly people tend to mumble the last few words of a sentence (and drop their voices at the same time) that they started off quite clearly.

Group activity

(*a*) Each member of the class prepares a short piece of writing (about 100 words from a book, magazine, newspaper) to read to the others. It is to be read principally from the point of view of audibility. At the beginning of each reading the class put up their hands. As soon as they realise that they are hearing the reader they drop their hands. They raise them again as soon as they cease to hear. The reader's aim is, of course, to get all the hands down and keep them down.

At the end of each reading the teacher asks: 'Was he *intelligible* as well as audible?' (i.e. did he articulate sufficiently well that everybody could distinguish what words he was reading?)

(*b*) Each member of the group in turn performs the action of some task well known to him (preferably to do with his work) while carrying on a running commentary.

Afterwards the group comments on his audibility. Specific points for the group to check: (1) Did talking and moving at the same time reduce audibility? (2) Were there moments when the audibility level dropped particularly sharply? (3) If so, why was this?

Exercise 2
Say the following loudly, as clearly as you can. Any sentence you have difficulty with should be repeated several times (at home as well as in class). This will give you practice in moving the organs of articulation quickly and accurately.

(*a*) In my opinion this recorder is distinctly superior to the one I showed you previously.
(*b*) Our credit facilities are temporarily discontinued.
(*c*) With whom did Scott make his expedition to the Antarctic?
(*d*) The sale of sheets is starting on the twelfth, isn't it?
(*e*) His favourite food is fried fish fingers with chipped potatoes.
(*f*) Hand me the hammer and sixteen angle brackets, Harry.
(*g*) I should feel ill after a meal of stewed eels.
(*h*) A little bottle of acetic acid and an automatic electric kettle, madam.
(*i*) She saw the ship sailing slowly past the shore.
(*j*) These statistics were prepared by the store's senior statistician.

Exercise 2 will probably have reminded you of various tongue twisters that you heard when you were a child. A couple of really teasing ones are *The Leith police dismisseth us* and *Do you know Peggy Babcock*? (The second of these should be attempted six times at speed to achieve maximum confusion!) There is no harm in trying a few of these in (and out of) class – it will provide practice in moving your organs of articulation quickly. But you must remember that tongue twisters are *designed* to tangle you up, and very few people (including the author of this book) can avoid being tangled up by them. Exercise 2 on the other hand, provides gentle exercise in the kinds of articulation movements that people tend to be careless over or find troublesome.

II. Stress

To emphasise certain words in the sentences we speak we give them greater weight (forcing through a little extra air for that word). Such 'stress' gives subtlety to speech, of a kind we can hardly imitate in writing at all. The whole meaning of a sentence can be altered by a change of stress.

Group activity
Speak the following sentences in various ways by putting the principal stress on each of the words indicated in turn (six versions of each sentence). Discuss the shifts of meaning that result and the circumstances under which each version might be used.

(*a*) I don't know how he pays for it.

   I: don't: know: how: he: pays

(*b*) At this store an assistant is not allowed to change sales goods.

   this: assistant: not: allowed: change: sales

(*c*) These jackets were all slightly faulty.

   these: jackets: were: all: slightly: faulty

III. Regional pronunciation RP

Young people in jobs – such as retailing, hairdressing, and hotel work – where they have to speak to customers a great deal often worry about regional elements in their pronunciation. It is true that in a few high grade stores, salons, hotels etc. it is advantageous to have a posh* accent (provided it is genuine – nobody wants the *It looks diveen on modom* kind of speech) but in most jobs a regional pronunciation matters only if it is so far from the normal that the listener cannot understand.

What most people mean by a 'posh' accent is what is sometimes called RP (Received Pronunciation). RP is the accent employed by the BBC for news bulletins and the more formal programme announcements. It is the normal accent of educated people in south-east England, one which has always enjoyed high prestige because of its association with London and the court. The accents of the older universities and the public schools being also based upon that of south-east England, RP has been looked upon not only as an indicator of geographical origin but as a badge of membership of the ruling class. As such it has tended to arouse antagonism among those who do not use it themselves, especially when it is suspected that the user does not employ it naturally. At the same time there has been a tendency for those who use RP to look down on those with regional

*This old-established colloquialism, only just becoming acceptable in writing, derives from the initial letters of PORT OUT STARBOARD HOME the most desirable, and expensive, cabin booking on the trip to and from India in the heyday of the British Empire.

accents. The position is now changing fast. The days when almost everybody in a position of authority either used RP or felt embarrassed because he did not use it are in the past. Since the mid-1950s there has been a huge upsurge of actors and entertainers of nationwide influence who are clearly not ashamed of their regional accents and see them rather as an essential part of their personalities.

If, however, you have a very broad regional accent (to such a degree that people feel that you are talking dialect) or a marked foreign accent (this includes the West Indian accent) this may seriously interfere with communication and you should work to change it. You may be well advised to go to special classes.

An amusing exception to the general rule that a foreign accent is a handicap is the restaurant trade where the high prestige of continental food puts a foreign accent at a premium. As a result you will sometimes find a waiter who is perfectly capable of speaking clear English deliberately preserving his Spanish or Italian accent. Male hairdressers also seem to find a foreign accent something of an advantage (provided it is a continental one).

A slight regional accent is felt by many people today to give character and charm to the voice. It is noticeable that regional accents – if fairly marked – are more despised in their own home region than anywhere else. The further you go from home the more people will find interesting or attractive the accent that at home was considered 'low' or 'common'. On the other hand a very slight local accent is an advantage when you are working in the area of your upbringing – people feel you 'belong' and they can trust you.

It is best not to worry much about your accent provided people seem to understand you but to concentrate on volume, clarity of articulation, having a pleasant tone, and suiting your words and manner to the situation and the Rx.

IV. Tone

Your tone of voice affects your efficiency as a communicator. Your tone, for instance, may make you seem bad-tempered or bored or conceited. Some assistants in stores sound *supercilious* (as if they were looking down their noses at the customer); others sound *condescending* (as if they were doing a great favour in serving this half-witted customer); others again sound *obsequious* (as if they are crawling to the customer to get him to buy something). It is easy to antagonise the Rx by tones of this kind. On the other hand a warm, friendly, lively tone will help to establish a good relationship between assistant and customer. Communication is improved as a result.

The 'pitch' of your voice (i.e. they way your voice moves up and down on a musical scale as it were) affects tone. If you speak with very little variety of pitch the result is a monotonous and dreary voice. You will sound as if you are bored (whether you are or not) and you will therefore bore your Rx and he will not listen to you with much concentration.

Part of the art of good speech is to sound interested and enthusiastic, even if you are not – even if it is the end of a long and trying day.

Exercise 3

(a) Record on a tape recorder a brief talk about something that really interests you (e.g. your hobby, your holiday plans, your favourite sport, your favourite singer), or a reading of a passage or poem that you find exciting, or moving, or very funny.

On playback, listen to hear (1) how clearly you speak, (2) how interested you sound.

(b) Record something that does not interest you very much (the route from your home to the college, the syllabus of the course you are studying, an extract from a textbook) and try to make it sound interesting and pleasant to listen to.

V. Organisation

If our Rx is to understand us easily we have to organise our ideas sensibly. The linear nature of language affects us even more when we are communicating by speech than it does when we are writing, because the Rx has no chance to rearrange what we have told him. What has been *written* he can reread and puzzle over until he has straightened out the imperfections of the way we have passed on our information. What is *spoken* has gone for ever once it has been uttered and a bad order of ideas can make the information almost incomprehensible. Even quite short material – such as an announcement over a public address system, or a reply to an enquiry at the counter about an item on sale – needs to be arranged in logical order. This means that whenever it is possible we should take a few moments to organise what we have to say before we start to say it.

We should perhaps start off by making sure how much the Rx already knows about what we have to tell him. This may involve asking one or two questions. Then we should sort out what we have to tell him so that one point leads to the next in a logical order. We should take care to avoid irrelevant points that clutter up his mind with material he does not really need to know.

We cannot do this organising as we go along, unless we are very experienced at this sort of thing. Usually when we are speaking to people we have only a few moments to collect our thoughts and arrange them; we have to get used to doing it fast. If the material is very complicated it may be necessary to jot down the points you have to make on paper, even if this does mean keeping your Rx waiting for your reply to his query. When you are answering the telephone and have some time in advance to prepare what you have to say, this is certainly worth doing unless what you have to say is quite straightforward. If you have to make a speech or give an oral report, you should always prepare outline notes first.

Group activity A
Students take it in turn to make a short announcement to the class. The class then comments on its audibility, articulation, tone, order of information. A few suggestions for subject matter follow. For (*a*), (*b*) and (*c*) the announcer must pretend that the class does not know this information already.

(*a*) What break arrangements are for the class and where refreshment can be obtained.
(*b*) When the college library is open and how you can borrow books from it.
(*c*) Procedure in the event of fire (based on college fire precautions for the classroom but not simply read from them).
(*d*) An (imaginary) student meeting for the next day – when, where, what about, who should attend.
(*e*) The arrangements for an (imaginary) educational visit or theatre trip.
(*f*) Some possession has been lost by a student (not the announcer) on the premises – what, where, when believed to be lost, to whom a finder should hand it.

Group activity B
Here is Angela, the dazzling, but slightly muddleheaded blonde in the Registrar's office at Pidderminster College, who has been put on Enquiries because the regular girl is away sick, telling a new student how to get to the Shanklin Street Annexe.

'It's easy to get to the annexe. You just go down Silver Street to that corner shop – what's its name? – the shoe shop. Jill, what's that shoe shop called? You know, the one where you got those red sandals in the sale last summer. Cor, did they? I bet your feet looked funny. Did you take them back? Well, I would have. I mean to say, sale or no sale you don't expect them to do that, do you? Well, what's it called then? Oh yes, Duxbodys. Yes, that's it. Well you turn right at Duxbodys and then left again into another road. That's Shanklin Street. I mean the road you get into after you turn left is. You turn left again in Shanklin Street you see. The annexe is right at the end on the left. It's an old school. Well, that's the front of it. You won't be allowed in there. Students have to go in through the side entrance. That's in Cambridge Street. You go across the front and turn left. That's Cambridge Street. Come to think of it Cambridge Street comes out on to Silver Street further down just past Woolworths. You'd do better really to go down Silver Street to Woolworths and turn right just past.
    'Oh, don't you know Silver Street? I thought you'd have known that! Well, you know where the No. 10 buses go down? Oh, you don't know how to get there from here? Well, you go out through the front door and turn right outside. Well, not exactly right because that goes into the car park but sort of crooked ways right. Past the fountain. Well, when you come on the the road there's two roads come together opposite you. You take the righthand one – righthand if you've got your back to the fountain I mean, of course – and follow it down to

Silver Street. You'll recognise Silver Street because of the traffic lights. You turn left in Silver Street and that shoe shop I was telling you about is about a hundred yards down on the right.'*

(*a*) Discuss Angela's effort.
(*b*) Work out together a more effective version of her directions. (What question should she have asked first?) Don't forget she is speaking not writing: what you write must sound like speech.
(*c*) The class selects one member to record the group version.
(*d*) Discuss the new version after it has been played back to you.

Group activity C
The group divides equally into 'sales assistants' and 'customers' and pair up. 'Sales assistants' prepare a product (for example – cheese; all the better known varieties, their differences, appearance, the price range etc.). The 'customer' prepares three or four questions to ask about his/her partner's product. The pair then act out in front of the class an impromptu sales situation, the 'customer' asking questions and the 'sales assistant' replying until a sale results. This must not be rehearsed – in fact the 'customer' must not reveal in advance to the 'sales assistant' what questions he is going to ask.

The situation can, of course, be adapted to take place in a restaurant, hairdressing salon etc.

Exercise 4
1. Select one of the situations (*a*) – (*e*) below.
2. Write out what you would say (and remember it is speech not writing).
3. You should not attempt to learn this by heart – but when your turn to speak comes you will know roughly what you want to say, although you will probably use slightly different words from those in your written version.
4. To get full value from this exercise the spoken version should be taped (i) to compare with your written version, (ii) for self-criticism, (iii) for group criticism.

(*a*) You are showing a visitor round the college (or a part of the college), round your store, warehouse or other place of work (only about one minute of this required i.e. 100-120 words).
(*b*) You have to give an oral report of an accident (street, or at work) that you have witnessed (invented details will probably be needed).
(*c*) You are describing to the boss the symptoms of an illness that a workmate/customer is suffering from (invented details will probably be needed).
(*d*) You have to describe clearly to your employer how you get to your place of work from your home/the college/the railway or bus station (whichever is the most complicated).
(*e*) You are to describe to the class some product of high quality or some possession that you prize highly.

* Reprinted from Little, *English for the Office.*

NOTE. The above exercise can with profit be carried out twice to enable students to learn from their first-time mistakes. Students should perhaps make their own choice of situation the first time round but be detailed to a particular one by the teacher the second time (the situations are not equally demanding).

VI. Tact

Tact in communication is a matter of considering the feelings of the Rx, of putting what you have to say in a way that will not ridicule, hurt, offend, or anger him/her. It is desirable in all forms of communication but is particularly necessary (and particularly often conspicuously absent) in oral communication with customers.

Lack of tact does not so much affect the passing of the message (that may be only too clear to the customer) – it affects vitally the response aimed at. By tactlessness you can quite easily turn the person to whom you are attempting to sell goods or a service into somebody who will never deal with you or your firm again. The hairdressing assistant who says: 'You are going a bit grey, Madam. Why don't you try a colour rinse?' is not very likely to sell the customer the rinse, which is the response she is aiming at. On the contrary she may well lose her tip and – more important – the salon employing her may lose a good customer. The wine waiter who clumsily shows up the customer as one who does not know what wine to order is not likely to see that customer again. It is perfectly possible to guide an inexperienced customer by hints to choose a wine that he can afford and that will go well with the food he has ordered. A customer skilfully handled in this way will often show his immediate appreciation by an above-average tip – and even if he does not, the tactful waiter has the satisfaction of having done his job well and avoided spoiling a customer's evening by making him look, or feel, a fool.

Hairdressers, hotel receptionists, waiters and waitresses, sales assistants, etc. have endless opportunities to make customers feel stupid, old, tired, poor, badly dressed, ignorant, unfashionable, plain, unshapely, and generally inferior. They also have endless opportunities to make customers feel rather pleased with themselves, to feel that they are not quite so stupid, old, tired etc. as they thought they were when they entered the salon, hotel, restaurant, shop, or store. From the point of view of successful communication there is no doubt which response should be aimed at.

In the 1930s there was a stock saying – *The customer is always right.* A buyer's market and massive unemployment resulted in humiliating crawling to customers. A complaint from a customer often led to immediate dismissal, and another job was almost impossible to obtain. Nobody wants to see those days back again. But it does sometimes seem that the pendulum has swung too far the other way and that nowadays the customer is always wrong.

It is certainly strange that so many people whose job is dealing with customers speak to them with such brutal lack of tact; it is almost as if they *want* to offend those on whom, after all, their livelihood does depend. The short article that follows is typical of many that have been appearing in the national press over the last few years.

What is it that makes women who might be very pleasant and polite anywhere but in a shop feel that they can say anything to you because you're a customer? The worst insult I ever had was from a frozen-faced, snooty, floor superintendent in a large shoe store. Steely eyes swept me up and down as she said: 'Nothing 5 under £5 in this department.' As a matter of fact, I could have paid £5. Or more. So there. But I turned on my (admittedly rather run-down) heels and walked out. I don't mind too much when, as frequently happens, a dress shop assistant tells me how slimming the lines are, even if it has not occurred to me that my curves 10 need hiding. After all, she means well. But I do object to the lazy excuse for never having snappy styles in anything but dwarf sizes: 'They're really not the thing for bigger women, madam.' All too often, the real reason is that there's been an enormous run on the few models for the not-so-stunted which the shop has bothered to 15 stock. Little women make good targets, too. A mature but attractive friend, lean as a whippet, was slung out of a dress department by an assistant who didn't happen to have what she (perfectly reasonably) wanted, with the bitchy murmur: 'This department is really more for the *jeune fille,* madam.' Wandering 20 to a cosmetic counter, she got another, and almost literal, slap in the face. One of those beauty experts with an unreal Japanese-mask make-up face was demonstrating before a crowd of women. My friend idly picked up a pot of the cream which was being blobbed on a youthful model's face. Quick as a flash, Japmask 25 said loudly: 'Oh, that's not for you, madam. Now, over here we have a much heavier cream which will conceal all the tiny lines and blemishes of the more mature skin.' Then there is the evidence of another friend, who bounced into a shop to buy a coat. Peeling off her old one, she said cheerfully: 'I bought that 30 one here.' 'Yes,' said the assistant, eyeing the crumpled heap coldly, 'from our cheaper department.'

Gerda Paul in *The Daily Telegraph*

1. (*a*) How many separate examples of tactlessness are mentioned here?
   (*b*) List them.
2. Because this is rather informal newspaper writing the author uses a number of colloquialisms that would not be acceptable in more formal writing. List these. (You should be able to find at least five.)
3. In line 7 why does the author add *So there*?
4. In lines 21–22 reference is made to an 'almost literal' slap in the face. What would have to happen for it to be a literal slap in face?

For discussion
A. 1. What kind of customer will want to be called *Madam*?
   2. Is there any kind of customer who would prefer to be called *dear*?
   3. Is it correct for a young assistant to call *any* customer *dear* or *love*?

4. Are there any ways other than *Sir/Madam* to address a customer that will maintain a good communication relationship with the customer?

B. Many people pad out what they have to say with meaningless 'fillers' of which the most common are probably: *you see*; *you know*; *well*; *actually*; *like*. Some people have a particular addiction to one of these, putting in, perhaps, *you know* regularly after every few words. Others use several at once as in: *Well, you see, what actually happened was he was out checking the stock in the back of the shop, like, when this feller comes in, you know, and starts bashing about at all the bottles and stuff, like, that's on the display shelves with this hammer, you see.*

1. What similar fillers can you remember hearing?
2. Why do people talk like this?
3. Is any communication purpose served?
4. Are there communication disadvantages in talking like this? If so how can those who do it stop themselves?
5. Do you consider the use of *like* as in the example above in some way worse than using the other fillers? If so, can you decide why?
6. The kind of person who speaks this way also often uses *this* in a rather unexpected way. Find two instances in the example and discuss them.

6
Writing to Communicate

With this chapter we begin to concentrate on written communication. In your daily work you will be making much greater use of oral than of written communication. Communication outside your work will also be predominantly oral. You are probably therefore surprised to notice that more space is devoted to written communication in this book than to oral. The reason is quite simple: it is precisely because you get so much more practice in oral communication that you need more help with written communication.

How much use you will make of written communication in your work in the future (or whether you will ever have to write at all) depends upon how you are going to be employed. Very few readers of this book will be expected to write more than a word or two on a form of some kind in their present jobs. Promotion might change this position very considerably and the chance of promotion might rest on ability to handle simple written communication. As soon as you rise to a supervisor's position the need to be able to communicate accurately and easily in writing becomes apparent. If you rise to a managerial position you will find a large part of your working day devoted to written communication.

In learning how to communicate effectively in writing you are planning for the future, rather than acquiring a skill of immediate application to your work.

The range of written communication relevant to those working in the distributive trades extends from simply filling in forms – order forms, wants slips, receipts, bills of sales etc. – through postcards to customers, internal memos, showcards, short goods descriptions etc. to full-scale business communication including letters and reports.

It is not only for our work, however, that we need to be able to write a business letter or a simple report. A claim on an insurance company arising from a car accident, for example, requires both. We need to be competent in written communication as private persons as well as in our role as employees.

Our own language is our principal tool of communication. Once we have realised this we find ourselves looking at learning about how to use it effectively quite differently from the way we did during English lessons at school. We see, for example, that from the viewpoint of effective communication in a business situation, it is not so much *how* we write that matters, as *what we have to say* when we write. At work we never have to write just because somebody has told us to do so, as an exercise. We write because we have information somebody else needs, or because we are trying to obtain information, or action, from somebody. What really matters, therefore, is that the person at the other end 'gets the message'.

Similarly in our private lives, away from warehouse, shop, or salon, if we have to write something it is *for a purpose* – we are making arrangements to meet somebody, claiming on our insurance, complaining that we have been overcharged, ordering goods, booking a holiday, asking for a catalogue etc. If the Rx does not understand properly what we are writing about we are wasting our time writing.

How we write *does* matter of course – very much; but only in so far as the way we write:

1. helps the Rx to understand our message (always);
2. makes the Rx feel towards us the way we want him to feel (usually).

When we write to communicate, the kind of response we are aiming at from the Rx is not: *How beautifully this person writes. What a remarkable vocabulary he has! I am most impressed* – but something like: *Yes I understand what he is getting at and he seems a reasonable good-tempered sort of person.*

Communication aims in writing are therefore quite different from literary aims ('expression'). In school our English classes are (for excellent reasons) mostly devoted to self-expression; the examples put before us are usually literary ones, and most of the exercises in writing we attempt have literary aims.

For communication purposes we have to think quite differently about our use of English. We are writing for a purpose; our aim is to achieve that purpose in the minimum number of words that will permit us to be completely clear. Our goal is a plain one – to make it easy for the Rx to understand what we are telling him.

Six important steps towards this goal are as follows:

1. Know your Rx (see Chapter 2).
2. Get your thinking right before you do anything else. You can hardly hope to put your ideas down clearly on paper if they are not clear in your own head.
3. Plan, organise, arrange before you start to write, It is your job to see the Rx receives your information in logical order (see Chapter 4).
4. Write in soundly constructed sentences.
5. Divide longer material (say 150+ words) into paragraphs, to make it easier for the Rx to follow (or numbered sections if you are writing a report).
6. In converting your ideas/information into words try not to distort and do not waste words. At the same time remember what we have already stressed in Chapter 2 about suiting your language to the Rx.

Chapters 7 and 8 will help you with steps 4 and 5 respectively. Step 6 you should start putting into practice immediately and should remember whenever you have to do any speaking or writing. Detailed help with some special difficulties about choice of words is provided in the second half of this book (Chapter 16).

For discussion

To what extent do the following sentences communicate their message to you satisfactorily? Do not look at the notes that follow (upside down) until your discussion is complete.

1. Communication plays an important role in the distributive trades.
2. The purple pianos wriggled on their enamel mantelpieces.
3. I aint never received no goods and I aint gonna pay for goods I aint ad.
4. With reference to your order of 15th May 19.. for ten packets (100) manilla envelopes.
5. Renewal in existing town centres is often organic and comprises piecemeal reconstruction of individual sites.

NOTES ON SENTENCES (ABOVE) TO BE DISCUSSED–DO NOT READ BEFORE THE DISCUSSION HAS TAKEN PLACE

Sentence 1. You probably decided this sentence communicated well. You should note that for different Rxs it might have communicated very little as they may have had much less idea than you now have what *communication* means and may also not have been clear what *distributive trades* referred to. Would everybody know what *role* means in this sentence?

Sentence 2. A meaningless sentence invented by the author. Included to illustrate that a sentence can be completely *correct* and yet be valueless as communication.

Sentence 3. This is the reverse of 2 – a sentence that communicates quite clearly although full of errors that teacher's red pen would long to slash through.

Sentence 4. Not a sentence at all! (Why not?) Not much is communicated. There is also an ambiguity (double meaning). Were the packets of envelopes 10s or 100s?

Sentence 5. Extracted from a professional magazine of the building trades. You probably decided that this communicated very little. It would have conveyed its message fairly well to the usual readers of this magazine. You were the wrong Rxs for this sentence.

You will have discovered from your discussion that there are important differences between communicating and writing 'correctly' – and to communicate is much more important than to be correct.

What we speak is often 'incorrect' by school standards, but nobody has much doubt about what we mean; so we have communicated successfully. Similarly when we write we do not have to be correct to communicate. Nevertheless (in writing more than in speaking) it is desirable to be as correct as possible as well as communicating because the Rx may form an unfavourable opinion of us if we make many mistakes. You might say that the author of Sentence 3 above unconsciously communicates something about his standard of education and his social background as well as the message he is conveying. This might – with some Rxs – have the effect of reducing the seriousness with which his message is treated. Certainly, gross mistakes cannot be tolerated in letters and other written material coming from business houses; these are always expected to be of a high standard of correctness.

Exercise 5

Write an account of your job, in about 200 words, entitled 'My Job'. This is not an 'essay'. You should look on it as a real attempt to communicate the facts about your job to your teacher. He will want to know about this; it will enable him to teach you more effectively if he has the information.

Points to bear in mind include: how you came to take up this job in the first place; what you do; your prospects; your ambitions; where you work; how you like your job. These are not the only points that could be included and you do not have to include all of them – they are just starting points for you in thinking about what you are going to write. They are not given you in the best order either – part of the exercise is to decide what order you are going to put your points in.

Finally, have another look at the six steps listed on page 41 before you start writing.

7
Writing in Sentences

I. Sentence errors and communication

When your teacher had marked and returned Exercise 5 you probably found that one of the most widespread errors in the class was that what you had written had not been correctly divided into sentences.

When we write we must divide what we write into sentences, and indicate these by a capital letter at the beginning and a mark of ending at the end of each. There is no equivalent to this when we are talking. We do not speak in sentences all the time and we do not have to indicate (by a pause for instance) where our sentences end – although some careful speakers do in fact do this. As a result most people (because they speak so much more often than they write) tend to make errors in their sentence division when they write.

We saw in our discussion on page 42 that communicating is not just a matter of avoiding mistakes, and a soundly constructed sentence may be quite useless if it communicates nothing. It is also perfectly true that we may communicate fairly well even if we do make sentence errors, provided there are not too many of them. Nevertheless, the sentence is the basis of writing and if we do not handle our sentences properly we may make it difficult for the Rx to understand us. Furthermore, sentence errors are so widely considered a sign that the writer does not know how to write his own language that you will want to try to avoid making them.

To avoid sentence errors it is necessary (1) to know what a sentence is and (2) to have some rules by which to judge whether what we have written makes an acceptable sentence.

II. What a sentence is

The sentence is the basic unit of written language. This is true for all languages, not only English. It is the smallest unit of written communication that can stand alone.

Some of you will be surprised at this statement. If you had thought about it at all, you probably considered the word the basic unit. It is true, of course, that words can in a physical sense stand alone – we see them often enough in dictionaries and spelling lists. But in a communication sense a written word cannot stand alone unless it forms a sentence. Thus we would not normally know what message was intended if we received – in writing – from the Tx the word *sausages* and nothing more. We would assume it was only part of a sentence – that might have read: *Sausages are my favourite food* or *Please send me some more sausages*.

In speech it is different:

MUM: *What would you like for tea?*
JOHN: *Sausages.*

Here *sausages* can stand alone and give a complete message to the Rx (Mum).

For discussion
A. Which of the following are sentences? How do you know?

1. He fried the sausages in lubricating oil.
2. All the sausages split.
3. The sausages, although he had fried them very carefully and pricked them with a fork before putting them in the pan.
4. Hissed and spluttered merrily in the bubbling oil.
5. He fried the sausages in lubricating oil, all the sausages split.
6. The sausages were fresh.
7. Were the sausages fresh?
8. With reference to your account of 15th May on which three items were omitted.
9. The full details of our autumn special offers, including discounts for cash sales.
10. NO PARKING.

B. What is a sentence?

You probably had a confusing sort of discussion about what a sentence is, and found you all had rather different ideas. This is not surprising as grammarians have produced over two hundred definitions of the sentence over the years. The trouble about most of these definitions, some of which you probably met in school, is that they do not help you very much when you are trying to decide whether what you have written is a sentence or not. The most useful definition is one that draws attention to the sentence's ability to stand alone.

A sentence is a unit of writing complete in itself, i.e. not by grammatical construction part of another unit.

Thus, of the sentences and non-sentences you have just been discussing, *All the sausages split* is a sentence. It is complete in itself, not part of something else. *The sausages, although he had fried them very carefully and pricked them with a fork before putting them in the pan* is part of another unit the exact words of which we cannot know but which may have read, for example: *The sausages, although he had fried them very carefully and pricked them with a fork before putting them in the pan, split.* It is therefore not a sentence.

Sentence errors are of two kinds:

1. putting between capital letter and mark of ending a group of words that the Rx cannot accept as a sentence;
2. jamming two sentences together without any grammatical structure to link them.

The two types of error are looked at more closely in sections III and IV.

For discussion
1. Amongst the sentences and non-sentences you have been discussing there were several examples of the first type of sentence error but only one example of the second type. Which was that?
2. How many 'marks of ending' are there in English?

III. Conventional sentences

Everybody using this book will have been given rules of some kind at school by which to write sentences. There are almost as many versions of these rules as there are definitions of the sentence, and none of them are completely satisfactory. The version that follows is as satisfactory as any, and has the advantage of requiring the minimum of grammatical knowledge.

EVERY SENTENCE MUST CONTAIN TWO PARTS.

One part THE SUBJECT, draws the attention of the Rx to the person, thing or idea that the sentence is about.

The other part, THE PREDICATE, may be one of three kinds:

1. tells the Rx what the subject did (or does or will do);
2. tells the Rx what happened to the subject (or is happening or will happen);
3. provides the Rx with further information about the subject, using the verbs *be, have, seem,* or *appear* and a few similar verbs (i.e. not involving action).

Some examples follow:

SUBJECT	PREDICATE	
All the sausages	*split*	(Type 1)
He	*threw the sausages away*	(Type 1)
The sausages	*were thrown away*	(Type 2)
The sausages	*appeared to be ready*	(Type 3)
The sausages	*were fresh*	(Type 3)

Orders, instructions, demands, requests etc. ('imperatives') are something of an exception. The Rx is himself the subject (i.e. when the Rx reads *Turn the knurled wheel fully clockwise before operating the grinder* he knows *he* is the one who is to do the turning; when the motorist sees the sign *HALT* he knows *he* is the one who is supposed to halt.

Similarly in speech, when we want somebody to do something we do not always find it necessary to name him. We say things like: *Pass me the hammer, Stop doing that!, Turn right outside the store and go down as far as the traffic lights.* With imperatives, therefore, the subject is not always expressed – it is the one way you can have a conventional sentence that has only a predicate.

Normally the subject precedes the verb of the predicate as in all the examples given above. Sometimes this is the only way that we know which *is* the subject out of two possible nouns. In *Harry hit John*, word order is the only indication which one is doing the hitting. Reversal of this normal order produces the question form – *Were the sausages fresh?*

You should note, however, that for special effect the normal word order is sometimes changed – to add emphasis or improve rhythm in a sentence, perhaps. For example:

PREDICATE	SUBJECT
Down came (Type 1)	*the rain*

Labels and headings are worth a moment's attention. These do stand alone but they are not sentences (as they lack the two parts). If you have behind your counter a number of trays marked *Shirts, Socks, Cravats* etc, these labels are quite clearly not sentences. Similarly verbal signs such as *NO PARKING* are not sentences.

A few lines back (at the end of the paragraphs on imperatives) reference was made to 'conventional' sentences, i.e. ones that keep to the rules and are acceptable to everybody. In literary writing and advertising we see today many unconventional sentences. Poets and novelists have over the last thirty or forty years carried out a good deal of experimenting with what are sometimes called 'fragmented' sentences (i.e. part sentences). Copywriters have seized on these fragmented sentences as a way of giving extra zest to their advertising writing. The mattress advertisement on the following page is a typical example.

Exercise 6
(a) How many conventional sentences are there in the mattress advertisement?
(b) Rewrite it in conventional sentences throughout.
(c) Compare your version with the original and then write down in one (conventional) sentence why you think the copywriter wrote the way he did.

At work (unless you are asked to write advertising copy) and in examinations, you should keep to conventional sentences. That fragmented sentences are used so much in advertising makes it harder for students like yourselves to avoid sentence errors. However, you cannot excuse breaking the rules in formal business writing by arguing that you

If you think your mattress supports your whole body, take a look inside

Most mattresses look as if they're supporting you all over.

On the surface.

But it's a different story inside.

Because a mattress that supports you on springs and wires can never be holding up every inch of your body.

While a Dunlopillo mattress can. It's made from the newest material to be used for mattresses—foam.

Every inch of it works to hold up every inch of you. Giving you the kind of continuous, all-over support a conventional mattress could never provide.

Foam can be made firm. Or soft. Or in between. You'll find the right firmness for you in our range of fourteen models.

A foam mattress airs itself, so it stays fresh, keeps you fresh, and never needs turning.

It's light, too. So you needn't break your back when you need to make or move it.

And talking of backs, did you know specialists recommend Dunlopillo foam mattresses for back-sufferers who need a firm bed?

So send for our catalogue and take a close look at the most advanced of modern beds.

(They cost from around £25 to around £150, for sheer luxury.)

That is if you want a bed that actually does what it seems to be doing on the surface.

were trying to write in fashionable fragmented sentences. When somebody reads a letter that starts: *With reference to your account of 15 May on which three items were omitted.* he knows perfectly well that the full stop is there not as a result of some experimental use of language – but because the writer does not know what a sentence is.

Exercise 7
Convert the following subjects into sentences by adding predicates at least four words long where the dots indicate.

1. The cigarette end . . .
2. Many customers . . .
3. Communication . . .
4. My great weakness . . .
5. The principal requirement in a sales assistant . . .
6. Pop music . . .
7. . . . the area manager.
8. Who . . .?
9. Swinging nimbly from branch to branch, the monkey . . .
10. Ladies and gentlemen, I . . .

Exercise 8
Convert the following into sentences by adding an appropriate subject at least three words long.

1. . . . fell down the stairs.
2. . . . was awarded a prize.
3. . . . turned out to have lost the receipt.
4. . . . asked for the trousers to be changed.
5. . . . is the most useful thing I learned at school.
6. . . . knocked the policeman's helmet off.
7. . . . decided that the gloves had been dirtied by the customer herself.
8. . . . has a built-in aerial.
9. . . . is a useful skill to have.
10. . . . is bound to become an important problem in the future.

Exercise 9
Simple sentences of the sort we have been considering are very successful commercially as slogans. Slogans should be brief, easy to understand, and easy to remember. Here are three well established examples that must each have, between them, stimulated sales worth many hundreds of thousands of pounds.

SUBJECT	PREDICATE	
Persil	*washes whiter*	(Type 1)
Guinness	*is good for you*	(Type 3)
(Rx)	*Go to work on an egg*	(Imperative)

Make up your own slogans for the following products. Do not copy ones that already exist. You may either use an actual product name or invent your own.

vacuum cleaner, car, soft drink, raincoat, anti-perspirant, washing-up liquid, perfume, lubricating oil, toothpaste, clear adhesive tape

IV. Sentence division

The opposite error to writing incomplete sentences is failing to stop and put a mark of ending when you come to the end of a sentence. As a result of this two (or more) sentences are jammed together, perhaps with a comma between. In extreme cases all the sentences run into each other and there is hardly a full stop to be seen.

People seem to do this less often when the subjects of the sentences thus run into each other are different than they do when they are the same. Thus fewer people would write: *He did not take sufficient care in nailing up the crate, the goods fell out in transit* than would write: *He was in a hurry to nail up the crate, he hit his thumb with the hammer.* A moment's thought will show that the structure of both these 'sentences' is identical (subject, predicate, comma, subject, predicate) and if one is wrong both are wrong. In fact, all constructions of this pattern are wrong.

Exercise 10
If any of the following do not seem to you satisfactory as sentences rewrite them.

(*a*) His bowler hat blew off, the elephant stepped on it neatly.
(*b*) The elephant, the bowler hat firmly attached to its foot, its trunk swinging briskly.
(*c*) In reply to your letter of 15 May in which you complain that the assistant on our gloves counter was impolite to you.
(*d*) The gloves were of suede leather, attempts to wash off stains always result in permanent marking of suede leather unless it has been specially treated.
(*e*) Let me have details of your requirements before 15 May.
(*f*) The manager checked the stocks himself, he found many items unaccounted for.
(*g*) Clear marmalade, full of the concentrated goodness of the whole fruit set in a natural marmalade jelly.
(*h*) Should be stored in a dry well-aired place when not in use.
(*i*) Storage compartment for microphone and accessories located on righthand side.
(*j*) Avoid excessive lubrication, it will cause slipping in the mechanism and possible stalling.

Exercise 11
Write out the following, dividing it into sentences correctly by adding capital letters and using suitable marks of ending where necessary. Some of these marks of ending may replace wrongly used commas. Do not change

the wording. Do not omit *necessary* commas. Retain your version when it has been corrected – you will need it for a subsequent exercise.

Tea is the dried leaves of a shrub called *camellia thea* the plucked leaves are spread out until half the water is dried out, next they are rolled by special machinery, then comes the fermentation stage during fermentation the colour of the leaves changes to brown, finally fermentation is halted by drying this process gives us black tea, the kind most of us drink green tea is not fermented a third type, Oolong, is half fermented all types of tea are sorted into sizes the smallest are considered best another grading divides leaf from broken tea in the beginning we obtained all our tea from China, now most of it comes from India and Ceylon it comes as 'originals' – unblended teas the tea-tasters make up blends that will appeal to customers some grocers who specialise in teas stock unblended teas four unblended Ceylon teas – Uva, Aurawa Eliya, Dimbula, and Kandy – are quite widely sold tea-bags are popular nowadays, they prevent tea-leaves getting into the cup they have the further advantage that they go into the wastebin afterwards and the sink is not blocked up with tea-leaves, they can also be used as compresses for tired eyes who would have thought it.

8
Writing in Paragraphs

For discussion

1. How do we indicate, when we are writing, that we have changed to a new paragraph?
2. How do we know when a new paragraph is necessary?
3. Why do we use paragraphs at all? (Try to imagine this book written without any paragraphing. Would it be harder to read and understand? If so, why?)
4. Is there any equivalent to paragraphing when we are speaking?

During the discussion that opens this chapter you will have found out for yourselves a good deal about why and how paragraphs are used. You will see that the need for them springs from the linear nature of words (see page 21). The Tx is forced to give information to the Rx in bits one after each other. If he gives him these bits of information in just any sort of order, as they come into his head, the Rx becomes muddled. It is clearly sensible to try to group together the bits that seem to belong together – give the Rx those – make a pause – then go on to the next group of bits. This is what paragraphing is. It is not merely a matter of chopping up our information into conveniently sized pieces – we also want the Rx to feel when he reaches the end of a paragraph that he has reached the end of one small complete part of what we have to tell him. We call these small complete parts 'topics'. The pause between paragraphs gives the Rx time to absorb what he has read and think about it before going on to the new topic in the next paragraph.

The one really important rule of paragraphing is therefore: *one topic, one paragraph*. If we try to deal with two unconnected topics in the same paragraph the Rx becomes confused. He also becomes confused if we divide one topic between two paragraphs. When he comes to the second paragraph he is *expecting* something different, not more about the same topic. Paragraphing errors of this kind are more worrying to an educated well read Rx than to one of a lower standard of literacy, because the more we read the more we expect paragraphs to follow the rule.

Unfortunately, in two areas of writing that users of this book are likely to be more familiar with than they are with most kinds of writing –

newspaper items and advertising copy – the rule is not strictly observed. For this kind of writing, material is often broken up into very small paragraphs to encourage easy reading even if it means dividing one topic between several tiny paragraphs, sometimes only one sentence long. Such writing is not a good guide to paragraphing for general business use.

Paragraphing is essentially a device for dividing up long pieces of written communication into sections of a length convenient for the Rx to absorb. Users of this book will seldom have occasion to write at great length; but you need to know about paragraphing even for quite short pieces of writing. Business letters, for example, are divided into paragraphs (unless they are only a few lines long). If you have to prepare a piece of writing as short as 100 words you need to know whether it can be left as one paragraph or whether (because it clearly includes two topics) it should be written out as two.

Exactly what constitutes a topic varies according to the length and scope of the total piece of writing. Quite small items can be built up to become topics if you are able to devote sufficient words to them; on the other hand if you are writing something pretty short but covering a wide subject matter paragraph topics have to be very broad.

For example, if an author was preparing a 1000 word article on 'Wool Production' for a geographical magazine he might well have one paragraph on the various kinds of sheep (such as Merino, Southdowns, Scottish Blackface) and the different types of wool they yield. If he was writing for a farming magazine an article of 4000 words on 'Growing Wool for the Modern Market' he would probably need to have a paragraph for each kind of sheep. If instead we consider a student writing a 400 word essay on 'Wool' the most space that he would be able to devote to kinds of sheep would probably be one sentence in a paragraph the topic of which was *Growing wool*. (Other paragraph topics might be *Wool through the ages*; *Manufacturing wool fabric*; *The uses of wool*.)

When you decide how you are going to paragraph what you write you are in fact doing one of two things (or sometimes a little of both). Either you are dividing up your total material into suitable sections or you have a number of small points too insignificant to merit a paragraph each which you have to sort out into groups so that each group of points makes up a topic. This will have a familiar sound to it; you will realise you have met this sort of approach to planning before. Paragraphing is an application of the principles of analysis and classification already discussed in Chapter 4.

The rest of Chapter 4 is also highly relevant: deciding the best order of presentation. This affects paragraphing in two separate ways. First you need to work out the best order to put your paragraphs in. Second, you have to consider the best order for the individual sentences that make up any one paragraph. In both instances, 'best' means best for the Rx, the order that makes it easiest for him to understand you.

Exercise 12
The following passage is printed as one paragraph. Do you think this is the way it was originally written – or should it be in two, or three, paragraphs?

If you think the passage should be divided into more than one paragraph indicate (1) where the division/s should take place (2) what the topics of the new paragraphs are.

If you think the passage is all one paragraph, what is its topic?

Increasingly, manufacturers are controlling the retail trade in various ways (usually cutting out the wholesaler in the process). Some own shops themselves, others tie the retailer to selling their products only, and not their rivals', by offering special discounts or other inducements (most petrol stations are an example of this). There may come a time when the retailer is on a more equal footing with the much-advertised manufacturer. Amalgamations of retailers diminish competition between them, but add to the retailer's strength in dealing with manufacturers. Already Great Universal Stores controls much of the retail furnishing trade; Debenhams controls about a hundred provincial department stores; and more such giant groups are likely to emerge, and to hold a strong bargaining position *vis-à-vis* the manufacturer. To a lesser extent, some big retail groups are beginning to control the activities of manufacturers – either outright or by laying down specifications to which they must produce. Marks & Spencers are the outstanding example of this.

Elizabeth Gundrey: *Your Money's Worth*

Exercise 13

The following passage has been printed without paragraphs. 1. Indicate where the paragraph divisions should come. 2. Name the topics of the paragraphs.

Look at the wool clothes which you see people wearing. Look, too, at the wool fabrics in your home. What a lot of different kinds there seem to be. Yet there are really only a few main kinds. Each of these main kinds of wool fabrics may be made in any one of a large number of patterns. They may also be dyed different colours, and given various special effects. Two of the most important classes of fabric are woollen and worsted cloths. Worsted cloths are made from yarns or threads in which the wool fibres are more or less parallel. The shorter fibres, too, have been taken out. This makes the worsted yarn compact and smooth. As a result worsted cloth has a clearcut appearance. The pattern of the cloth is very distinct. Woollen cloths, on the other hand, are made from yarns in which long and short fibres are mixed up, higgledy-piggledy. This gives woollen cloth a fuzzy appearance. In addition, both woollen and worsted cloths are woven. This means that they have some threads running longways (the warp), and the others laced over and under them (the weft). Another class of fabric is woven with a third set of threads, as well as the warp and weft. This third thread is looped through the others, so that all the loops stick out on the same side of the fabric. This is what is called a pile fabric. You have often seen them, because carpets and plushes are pile fabrics. Knitted fabrics are made up of one single length of yarn. They have no warp or weft. That is why they can be knitted, as you know, from a ball of wool, containing just one long length of yarn. No doubt you have heard of felt. Many hats and floor coverings, for example, are made of felt. In felt the wool fibres are jumbled up and pressed into a firm sheet, instead of being spun into yarn and then woven or knitted. The making of each of these different classes of wool fabrics is an industry on its own. There are also the wool skin and wool furskin industries. You can see that there is not just one wool industry. There are several different wool industries. The British wool industries are the biggest in the world. During the last hundred years they have employed up to 300 000 people a year. In Britain, the most important wool industries are those of the West Riding of Yorkshire.

Adapted from P. A. Wells: *Wool*

Exercise 14
Read the following passage and answer the questions that follow.

By using much less salt in their brine many bacon curers are now selling a product containing more water. This is the reason why four-rasher men, who used to be justifiably accused of gluttony, now find that they have barely enough bacon left to consume alongside a decent slice of bread. The ratio of water in bacon has 5 changed substantially – it used to be 250 parts water to 100 parts dry residue; now it is 450 parts water to 100 parts dry residue. For our 'convenience' (and presumably to help them sell water, which is one of the cheapest raw materials) manufacturers have processed cheese to spread easily and sell very well. Anyone who 10 has watched it (when unwrapped) disappear in the dry atmosphere of the refrigerator can understand why – it is packed with water. Instead of 60 per cent dry matter which exists in farmhouse Cheddar there is only 40 per cent in the spreads, with much less fat (20 per cent of the dry matter instead of 48 per 15 cent in Cheddar). These days more and more potatoes are being consumed as dehydrated instant mash. In Britain potatoes are one of our main sources of Vitamin C and the dehydration process almost completely destroys this compound. Processors could quite cheaply replace it by adding a little ascorbic acid but so far 20 none of them seem to have taken this obvious step. If your children begin to get scurvy – you know the reason why. The major change which has taken place in bread over the past fifty years – the dominance of a few factory bakers at the expense of thousands of small local bakers – has produced a lack of character 25 and variety rather than any major change in constituents or drop in nutritional standard. Recently, however, many managements, scared by the drop in bread consumption, have been trying to increase their range and introduce more breads of positive character. 30

Adapted from an article in the *Daily Telegraph Magazine*

(*a*) The passage has been printed without paragraphs. Where should they have come? Name the topic of each paragraph.

(*b*) What is *gluttony* (line 3)? How can these men be 'justifiably' accused of it?

(*c*) Why is *convenience* (line 8) put between inverted commas?

(*d*) What is meant by a *dehydration process* (line 18)?

(*e*) What do *processors* (line 19) do?

(*f*) What is meant by *dominance* in line 24?

(*g*) What do you think the writer means by *character* (lines 25 and 30) in connection with bread?

Exercise 15

You should have retained your exercise on Tea from Chapter 7. Rewrite it now as a properly paragraphed article. You need not keep the sentences absolutely unchanged if you feel you can improve them, but be careful not to bring in sentence errors.

Exercise 16

(*a*) What is the best order for the four paragraphs of the student's essay on 'Wool' referred to on page 53?

(*b*) Here is an outline for a paragraph on *pillar boxes*. Rearrange these points in the most suitable order.

> Shape and size of pillar boxes.
> Where situated.
> Invented by novelist, Anthony Trollope, in 1857.
> How collection times are indicated.
> Description of mouth of pillar boxes.
> How letters are extracted from the pillar boxes.
> Why pillar boxes are red.
> The function of the pillar box.

(*c*) Write the paragraph.

(*d*) If you were writing a 1000 word article, 'The Work of the Post Office', would you take as a paragraph topic *Pillar boxes*? Give a reason for your answer.

(*e*) If your answer to (*d*) was *No* indicate whether you would include pillar boxes at all. If you would, what would be the topic of the paragraph you would include them in?

Exercise 17

If you rearrange the following sentences and write them out (not on separate lines) you will find you have produced quite an interesting paragraph about the manufacture of cocoa, complete with introductory sentence. Do not forget to indent the first sentence. When you have a correct version, read it through carefully noting how each sentence prepares the way for the one that follows as it should in a well arranged paragraph.

> They are then roasted in a drum-shaped oven to bring out the flavour.
> The tins are lidded and labelled by machinery and packed into cardboard boxes.

The nib is crushed and ground between steel rollers.

The liquid is poured into pots and put into a press which squeezes out some of the cocoa butter.

The first step in manufacturing cocoa is to sort and clean the cocoa beans.

The cocoa powder is weighed automatically into tins.

The cocoa butter melts, and a thick liquid comes from the rollers.

The roasted beans are next broken into small pieces.

The press cakes are crushed.

The shells are winnowed away to leave the most valuable part, the 'nib'. Hard 'press cakes' are left behind.

The crushed press cakes are ground to powder and sieved through gauze.

Exercise 18

Write a paragraph the first sentence of which is: *The counter in a shop has a variety of functions.* Here are a number of points you may wish to include. They are not in the best order for using in a paragraph.

A platform to mount displays. A table to wrap up goods on. A barrier between customer and stock. A surface to demonstrate goods on. A place to store stock in (*a.* under-stock *b.* displayed stock, if glass-fronted). A table on which to write out bills of sale and other documents. A place to stand the cash register.

Exercise 19

The following details of an extension of waiting restrictions on vehicles in the area near the large store where you are employed have been received from the local council. Rephrase them to make a well planned paragraph suitable for inclusion in the staff magazine. The first sentence of the paragraph should read *We have received details from the Council of an extension of waiting restrictions on vehicles, to operate from 1 March 19..., that will affect us.* Make sure you write in acceptable sentences throughout.

Prohibition of waiting at all times

Herd Street	Its whole length, that is from The Green northwards to where the A.345 divides.
Barn Street	Between The Green and trunk road, A.4.
Martin Street	North side. From its junction with The Green to its junction with Blowhorn Street.
	South side. From its junction with Stonebridge Lane with the exception of the lay-by outside the Old People's houses.
Blowhorn Street	Both sides for 15 m northwards from its junction with Martin Street.

Waiting limited to 45 minutes with return prohibited within 1 hour

Martin Street	The lay-by at the Old People's houses.

Exercise 20

Write a 200–250 word magazine article entitled 'Customers', giving special attention to paragraphing (you should write out in advance the topics of your paragraphs and use this as a plan). Think of the different types of customer and any special difficulties you met with in dealing with customers when you started. You might like to attempt a humorous approach.

If your lack of experience with customers prevents your attempting this article, you may write instead on 'How knowledge of communication principles can help in . . . .' (filling in the blank with the name of the trade you hope to enter or are just starting in).

9
Inter-medium Practice Work

Practice work A

1. Study the picture below.
2. Write out the following and add words to make a complete sentence:
   In my opinion, the most depressing feature of this street . . .
3. In two sentences try to explain how you think living in a street like this would affect you. Start your first sentence with *If I lived in a street like the one in the picture . . .*

Practice work B
The photographs above and on the opposite page, which were being used by an advertiser at the end of 1971 – illustrate how much clothes can communicate or seem to communicate, since it is the same men in both photographs.

1. For the photograph above complete a sentence beginning *We are* to indicate what their clothes seem to communicate about the young men.

You may add a second sentence if you need to. There have been changes of fashion since the photograph was taken - try to allow for this and think in terms of what was probably communicated in 1971
2. Repeat the exercise for the photograph above.
3. In one or two sentences indicate what sort of clothes you consider most suitable for the work you do (or are training to do).

Practice work C

1. Study the photograph below.
2. In one sentence say what in your opinion the man and woman may be thinking.
3. Write down what you think *either* the man might say to the woman *or* the woman might say to the man. Remember that although you are writing this it represents *spoken* words.
4. The photographer (Tony Sapiano) called this prize-winning photograph 'Man is Mortal'. Write down in one or two sentences why, in your opinion, he gave it that title.

Practice work D

The cartoon by Garland on the opposite page first appeared in the *Daily Telegraph*. It is a good example of non-verbal communication, words having been found necessary only for identifying the car.

Answer the following questions about it *in sentences*.

(*a*) What do the five traffic signs mean?
(*b*) What other indications of difficult driving conditions are included in the drawing?
(*c*) What does the cartoon as a whole communicate?

Practice work E

The teapot shown below probably seemed a brilliant labour-saving device to its inventor. In a paragraph of about 80 words explain what he must have thought would make it so successful and why he was wrong.

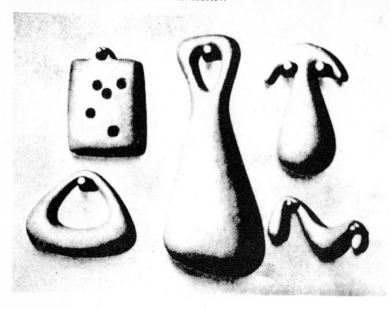

Practice work F

1. Study the picture above carefully.
2. Decide how you would describe each object.
3. Notice particularly how each object is placed in relation to other objects.
4. Decide what would be the most logical order in which to mention these objects in a description.
5. Write a one-paragraph description of the picture. All the objects must be included.

Practice work G

The two pictures opposite represent the view from the window of a cottage owned by the great eighteenth century garden designer, Humphrey Repton, before (upper picture) and after (lower picture) he replanned his own garden.

1. Make a list of the changes he made.
2. Number these to indicate what you consider the best order for inclusion in a paragraph about them.
3. Using this numbered list as an outline describe in a paragraph of about 150 words the principal changes Humphrey Repton made in his garden.

Practice work H
The four pictures below and opposite are very small reproductions of posters
aimed at reducing vandalism.

1. In one paragraph indicate which you think would be the most
   successful and which the least successful, giving your reasons.
2. Invent your own anti-vandalism poster and draw it. If you really cannot
   draw at all, describe in a few sentences what your poster would look
   like instead. You may use words instead of a picture (as poster (B)).

(A)

Who pays for this?

Let's Tackle Vandalism

YOUR PARENTS!

(B)

This poster
does not solve
vandalism.

YOU DO

By reporting
wilful damage to
your local council
or police.

(C)

(D)

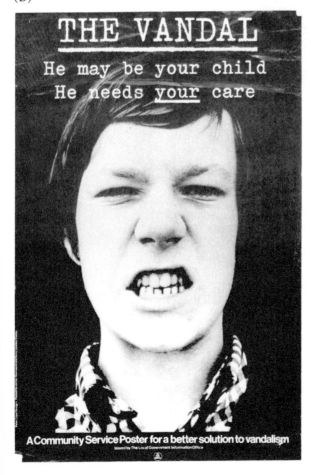

Practice work I

The porcelain teapot, cup and saucer, and jug above are part of a set designed by Luigi Coloni, a famous Italian designer, for Rosenthal. The jug has no handle and is intended to be just picked up. The handle of the teapot is incorporated in the body of the pot.

1. Write out about 20 words to be used on a showcard to be placed in front of this display in the store you work in. Do not attempt to include a price.

2. In about 80 words write out what you would say about this set to interest a customer who was looking at this display in your store. For this part of the exercise you should assume that there is no showcard. Remember that you are writing what you would *say*.

Part Two

10
Receiving Communication 1: Effective Listening

All through Part One we tended to concentrate on the transmitting end of communication. Responsibility for good communication does not, however, rest with the Tx alone. Communication is a twoway activity and the Rx must play his part too. A Tx can only be as successful in communicating as the Rx permits him to be. It is time now to look at the receiving end of communication, starting with listening.

The twoway nature of communication is seen more clearly in spoken communication – a game of tennis in which both Rx and Tx help to keep the ball in play. Ideally the two participants should take it in turns to serve (i.e. to be the Tx) but in some communication situations one person is forced to play the Rx role most of the time. Examples are when you are being given instructions (at college or at work) or when a customer is telling you exactly what he requires. In such situations your job as Rx is to keep quiet and listen. This does not mean that you are inactive. Effective listening in a communication situation is an activity.

When friends or relatives are chatting to us we may often not listen very carefully to what is being said. We tend to switch our concentration on or off according to how much what the person says interests us or catches our attention. Sometimes we practically stop listening altogether while politely trying to look as if we are still paying attention. This sort of approach to listening is quite inadequate for a communication situation (i.e. one where you either want to, or have to, receive the information being transmitted accurately and in detail).

In a communication situation you have, as Rx, to work hard at your listening all the time. If you do not you waste what effort the Tx may have put into transmitting his message clearly. You may even have to make up for a poor Tx by extra effort in your listening.

The starting point in becoming an effective listener is to recognise listening as active – positive – something you consciously *do*. It is not just a matter of keeping silent while the other person speaks and letting his voice flow over you.

Good listening depends on maintaining unbroken mental activity and concentration during the whole of the time that the Tx is giving you information. As the Rx it is your duty to follow, point by point, everything the Tx says. You have (1) to hear him; (2) to understand him; (3) to absorb and retain the information he has transmitted.

If you do not understand you must feed back your doubt to the Tx as soon as you have a chance. This may involve (1) asking him to repeat what he said that you did not understand (or perhaps did not hear properly); (2) asking him questions; or (3) if the message is important and complicated, repeating it back to him so that he can check that you have the right idea. You can introduce a 'recap' of this kind by some such words as: 'Let me see if I've got this straight. What you want me to do is . . .' or 'I am not sure I am quite clear about your complaint. Are you saying that . . .?' Incidentally, asking for a recap like this often has the result that the Tx greatly improves what he has to say on the second attempt.

Bad listening results from one of three causes (or a mixture of these).

1. The Rx is too passive, does not really make an effort to listen positively.
2. The Rx thinks of something else while the Tx is speaking (perhaps to do with his work, but perhaps just what he is going to do when he finishes work – equally unforgivable).
3. The Rx half listens, but is so eager to reply that he uses up much of his mental energy working out what he is going to say when it is his turn to be the Tx.

This third category of unsatisfactory listening can bring about complete breakdown of communication and much bad feeling. The sort of thing that happens is that the reply made by Brown, the original Rx (since he has only partially listened to Anderson, the original Tx) will not be completely relevant. Anderson will try to correct Brown's misunderstanding. Again, Brown will not listen fully because he is busy thinking what to say next. Furthermore he will not realise how astray his reply was and think that Anderson is being deliberately difficult or has changed his story. Tempers begin to fray and misunderstanding deepens at each exchange between the two of them.

In extreme cases this kind of bad listener wants to be the Tx all the time. Such people try to make all spoken communication a monologue, crushing any attempts by the other person to get his say in or interrupting as soon as the other has said a few words. They often use such phrases as 'Kindly let me finish', or raise a silencing hand to prevent the Rx from wrestling the Tx role from them. They are not really listening even when they do keep quiet for once. They are just silently rehearsing what they are going to say next.

The main thing therefore is to pay attention and keep paying attention. You must fight to prevent anything – noise, a stomach ache, the Tx's mannerisms or odd-looking face – distracting your attention.

You should watch the Tx while you are listening. You often learn a little extra by studying his facial expression and if you keep your eyes on his face you reassure him that you are listening. In fact if you *look* attentive you often improve the quality of the Tx's communication. The fact that you are so obviously concentrating on every word he says makes him measure every word carefully.

If what is being said to you includes details that you are likely to forget (name and address, dimensions, day of the week for delivery etc.) you should make a brief note (and make sure you do not lose it). If the information being given you is lengthy and complicated (and this includes lectures at college) you should make detailed notes.

Making notes when you are listening offers the following advantages.

1. The act of making the notes helps you to concentrate, and forces you to try to understand what is being said.
2. The Tx sees that you are taking notice of what he is saying. He often improves his communication when he sees you are taking notes, and becomes more factual leaving out emotional comment and irrelevancies (very useful when, for example, a complaint is being made).
3. You have a record of what was said that you can refer to later to refresh your memory, or if the Tx changes his story.

Making notes is an important part of the skill of receiving communication effectively. Notes should be brief, well laid out and organised, and easy to read at a later date. Some hints on note-making are provided in the next chapter.

Exercise 21

List the factors by which you would judge what sort of person a customer was who was talking to you so that you knew how to communicate with him/her most effectively.

Exercise 22
In 150–200 words describe some examples of bad listening that you have
noticed at work and/or college. Think about what you are going to include
and how you will paragraph it before you start to write.

11
Receiving Communication 2: Making Notes

We saw in the previous chapter how useful making a note can be in increasing the effectiveness of our listening. Note-making is often valuable also when we are dealing with written material. We may, for example, have a long and complicated letter in front of us, or a legal document such as a contract, or a manufacturer's technical leaflet about an appliance. First, writing the note forces us to decide which *are* the principal points and to get them into some sort of order. This helps us to understand and absorb what we have been reading. Second, the note is a useful reminder of the subject matter for the future that will probably save us the trouble of rereading the original material.

There are innumerable situations where the ability to make quick accurate notes is essential. To demonstrate this, here is a selection of ten of the most common note-making situations which may involve those using this book.

1. Orders, requests, complaints etc. by customers.
2. Making appointments.
3. Answering the telephone.
4. Receiving oral instructions from your supervisor (or other person in charge of your work).
5. Leaving details for somebody else who is going to take over from you on an unfinished job.
6. Making a plan for some piece of written communication.
7. Preparing an outline of what you want to say before tackling somebody about some important point, or making a speech, or talking on the telephone, so that you do not leave something out when you are speaking.
8. Making a record of what is said to you in an oral report, a talk, a lecture at college etc.
9. Making out a list or programme – for example of tasks that you intend to carry out – so that you do not overlook an item.
10. Making a record of anything you have read that you think you may need again in the future (in, for example, a letter, a report, an advertisement, a leaflet, a legal document, a newspaper or magazine or book).

You will see that it is really worth while to learn how to make notes properly. The following detailed hints should prove useful, but the essence of note-making is twofold: *(a) selecting the items to be noted; (b) using the minimum number of words.*

I. Keeping words to the minimum

1. To help in keeping the number of words used to the minimum, notes are not usually written in sentences but are in 'note form', a style that omits such little words as *the* and *a*.

In note form this sentence would become:

To help in keeping number of words used to minimum, notes not usually written in sentences – in 'note form' (omits such little words as the, a)

Notice the way brackets are used in note form when something is explained.

2. Further words are saved by:
(*a*) cutting away any words not essential to the main sense;
(*b*) changing the wording to give the same sense in fewer words;
(*c*) removing examples.

Thus our note of the first sentence of this section might become:

To save words, notes are not usually in sentences – note form omits little words.

The shorter your note the more difficult it becomes to understand later. You have to strike a balance between saving time and space, on the one hand – and making sure your note will make sense to you months later, on the other.

II. Shorthand and abbreviations

1. Shorthand is useful provided you can read it back without effort. You still shorten and compress your material though – verbatim shorthand reporting is not note-making.
2, Most people who write notes frequently use some abbreviations to save still more time and space. Private abbreviations that only you understand are of little use if you are going to pass the notes to somebody else, but can be valuable in notes solely for your own use. The following are widely used and you will meet them also in handwritten documents that you receive:
shd (should) *wd* (would) *cd* (could) *s.o.* (someone) *f.* (fairly) *v.* (very) *mod.* (modern) *ref.* (reference) *gen.* (generally) *info.* (information) $>$ (becomes) $<$ (comes from) *C20* (twentieth century).

III. Selection of points

Select what you decide to make a note of very carefully. Pick out the important points and put them in the shortest form that you will understand later. Addresses, dates, personal names etc. likely to be important should be put down accurately and in full. Omit irrelevant points and minor details.

IV. Arrangement

Notes should be arranged systematically. This means organising them according to the principles of analysis and classification discussed in Chapter 4. Ideally they should also be in logical order. You can sometimes improve on the order the original Tx chose if he is not very good at communicating.

Notes of oral material are very difficult from this point of view since you are usually making your notes while the person is speaking. It is often necessary to make rough notes at the time and sort them out into a better arrangement afterwards. This is something to bear in mind when taking notes in class. Although the majority of teachers will take great care to arrange their material in the order that is most suitable for you before they start, and present it in a systematic way so that your notes cannot help being systematic, there are exceptions.

V. Headings and emphasis

Make your notes easy to work through later by:

1. using headings (each new group of facts should have its heading) and subheadings;
2. numbering or lettering points for greater clarity;
3. underlining important parts;
4. writing out in block capitals technical and other unfamiliar words that you might later misspell.

VI. Examples

A note on the first ten lines of this chapter might come out something like this:

1. *Notes useful with written material as well as oral.*
2. *Two advantages of making notes of written material –*
    (a) *forces selection of principal points and aids understanding*
    (b) *serves as future reminder.*

Notice particularly (i) the way lettering and numbering have been used (ii) that the three examples (letter, legal document, leaflet) have been omitted.

A more detailed example follows.

1. Read the following article carefully.
2. Look at the notes on it that follow.
3. Try to work out for yourself how the notes have been arrived at from the original article.

(You will observe that the order of the notes is not quite the same as the original order. In some ways the notes are better organised than the original. If the author had written the notes first and the article from the notes, perhaps the article would have been easier to follow. Many people do in fact use notes in this way when preparing a complicated piece of writing or a speech.)

There seems little doubt that the next few years will see vast changes – perhaps the most sweeping since the Middle Ages – for the housewife and those working in the distributive trades.

For centuries the housewife has had only two choices of shopping area: the high street or town centre on the one hand and a few local shops (perhaps only one) where she lives. Today a third choice is becoming increasingly available: the out-of-town locale where a large shopping centre or hypermarket has been developed.

A hypermarket may be defined as an isolated large-scale store in a green fields location. It will probably have a floor area of some 7000 to 12 000 square metres or more, of which at least 60 per cent will be sales area. Broadly speaking this means that the average hypermarket takes up an area on which it would be possible to build over a hundred semidetached houses. Each hypermarket is accompanied by extensive car-parking facilities and a filling station.

Hypermarkets differ from ordinary shopping centres in another way. Except perhaps in one or two specialist shops or hairdressing salons leased out to individual owners, everything being sold is being sold by the one developer. This means that an unprecedented amount of power is centred on the retailing group owning the hypermarket – they are the only ones who decide what brands are to be sold and what prices are charged. Consumer protection organisations are worried about this as it must mean reduction in the choice available to the shopper and the disappearance of competitive pricing between rival shops close to each other. They point out too that the hypermarket is unsuitable for the elderly and those without cars.

This matter of use of a car means that – except amongst the increasing group of families who have two cars – the shopping habits of the population will have to change. Instead of going to the shops every couple of days, husband and wife will tend to go together once a week (most commonly on a Saturday) and buy not only a week's supply of perishables but also paint, timber, tools, garden items, furniture, bedding, books, light fittings, clothes etc., all under the one roof. The growing use of frozen food storage facilities in the home will further increase the tendency to make very large purchases at one time, even of such items as meat and prepared foodstuffs.

One of the great attractions for the consumer – apart from convenience – is supposed to be the lower prices that result from bulk purchasing and bulk buying. There are some points about this, however, that the average housewife customer tends to overlook. For one thing she is doing her own delivering. She is acting as her own shop assistant and using her own house as the warehouse in which goods are stored in bulk until she requires them. It is possible that when customers begin to realise that the lower prices also include a lower standard of service they will begin to move back again to the smaller individually owned shops.

HYPERMARKETS

1. Characteristics of h.

(*a*) *Isolated out-of-town locale – aimed at car owners*
(*b*) *Very large (7000–12 000 square metres floor area – 60% of this selling area)*
(*c*) *Includes car-parking and filling station*
(*d*) *Developer controls almost all selling – very few subleased shops*

2.   Effects of h.

(*a*) *Give an additional choice of shopping locale*
(*b*) *Shopping habits will change – weekly shopping by wife and husband together to buy wide range of goods under one roof*
(*c*) *Bulk buying (further encouraged by home frozen food storage facilities)*

3.   Advantages of h.

(*a*) *Convenience*
(*b*) *Lower prices through bulk buying and selling*

4.   Disadvantages of h.

(*a*) *Unsuitable for elderly or carless*
(*b*) *No deliveries – limited service*
(*c*) *Bulk bought goods have to be stored at home*
(*d*) *Control centred on developers means limited choice and no competition*

VII. Practice work

Exercise 23
The purpose of this exercise is to ensure that you become familiar with the differences between sentence form and note form.

A. Change the following sentences to note form.

(Example:
   No aspect of restaurant operation is more important than efficient planning of the entire establishment from the outset of the operation.
   No aspect of restaurant operation more important than efficient planning of entire establishment from outset of operation.)

1. A good waiter is always clean and tidy. He must give attention to his shoes, his shirt-front and collar, and his apron. His hands and nails are to be scrubbed frequently. He must be polite to the patrons, to his colleagues, and to his superior. He must carry out his duties noiselessly.

2. A hotel reception office is a busy place. The majority of guests arrive during the hours between mid-morning and mid-afternoon. The receptionist must treat each guest as an individual even though she is very busy. It is essential to deal with new arrivals promptly; they must not be kept waiting. If the telephone is ringing the receptionist must ask the guest to excuse her while she answers it. The ability to deal with more than one situation at a time without becoming flustered is an essential accomplishment for the receptionist.

3. Before the retailer can evolve his best layout he must decide to what extent he intends to adopt self-service or self-selection. Self-service is more suitable to some trades than to others and it has made the greatest headway in those shops selling heavily advertised, branded, and prepacked goods. Self-selection is a modification of self-service; assistance is available to help customers seeking advice but they are able to handle and examine goods and narrow down their choice before the sales assistant is approached.

B. Advertising copy, especially in 'small ads', is often in note form. Expand the following advertisements into full sentence form.

1. Part-time shop assistant required to work Mon. – Thurs. 1 pm – 6 pm. Good rates of pay plus free hairset weekly. Apply Freebodys, Market Street, Pidderminster.

2. VAUXHALL VICTOR 1600 1971 £170 spent last week on engine and gear box – not used since. M.O.T. Good tyres. Light blue. £435. Call 615 Queens Drive, Pidderminster, or telephone 21368.

3.   THE FOREST HOTEL
                      Good food every day of the week.
                       Three-course Lunch at £1.30
BAR SNACKS   FULL À LA CARTE MENU IN EVENINGS
             TRADITIONAL ROAST LUNCH SUNDAYS
        Free house   Central heated   Friendly atmosphere

Exercise 24
Read the following dialogue, putting yourself in the assistant's place. Write the note for Mr Tranter (who is senior to you).

Customer: I bought a teaset here a couple of months ago. Beginning of April it would have been. I'm afraid I've lost the bill. It was a Danish set. Green design on it. The firm's name was Dannor. You only had the one like it. When I bought it I asked the assistant to try to get me two extra tea cups. I'm always breaking the cups of my teasets. The dresser cupboard's full of saucers. He said he'd have to order them specially as they weren't a regular line and he'd send me a postcard when he'd got them in. Well, it's quite a time and I haven't had the postcard and I'm wondering if he forgot all about it. Or perhaps they're in and he's not sent the card. Or the card's gone astray in the post. You see what I mean?

Assistant: Yes, Madam. *Checks 'Orders in' shelves but, seeing nothing resembling these tea cups, returns to customer.*

Assistant: I'm afraid I can't see your tea cups, Madam. What did the assistant look like?

Customer: Oh, much older than you. Tall and thin. Very thick glasses. Gingery hair.

Assistant: That would be Mr Tranter. I'm sure he wouldn't just have forgotten about your cups, Madam. I'm afraid he's off sick at the moment, though. We're expecting him back tomorrow, but I shan't be here myself then. Awkward. I think in the circumstances the best thing I can do is leave a note for him to deal with this as soon as he gets in. I'll ask him to drop you a line and let you know what the position is. Could I have your name and address, Madam?

Customer: Yes, that seems best. Mrs D. Brown, 53 Hilltop Drive. Thank you for taking so much trouble.

Assistant: Not at all, Madam. I'm sorry you've had to call in like this.

Exercise 25

Read the following article carefully. Then make notes on it. Supply your own title and subheadings. Look for every chance to use numbering and/or lettering to provide a clear layout. Where you can list items, do so.

Whatever you want to find out there is almost certainly at least one book that will tell you what you want to know. The difficulty is to find what the book is called. A further difficulty is to be able to look at it without having to buy it, for none of us want to buy books we may wish to refer to for only a short time. The answer is a library. A library will not only aid you in finding out where to look for information in books but also allow you to refer to the book on the premises or even (with most of its stock) to borrow it to take away and read at your leisure.

As a student you are probably fortunate enough to have access to two libraries – your local public library and your college library. The second may be much smaller than the public library but the books will have been carefully selected for people like yourself; it is easy to get to; and you are not competing with the whole of the general public for a chance to get hold of the book you need, only your fellow students. You will usually be well advised to try your college library first and to move on to the public library only if the college one cannot immediately supply what you require. If you know what book you want but it is not in stock locally, both libraries can apply to bigger libraries to borrow a copy for you if you ask them.

Libraries also hold booklets, pamphlets, magazines, trade journals etc. and, sometimes, newspapers. These can be of great use in supplying up-to-date information. Books take a fairly long time to produce – at least eighteen months writing and nearly a year after that editing and printing – so that even a brand new book is likely to be about a couple of years out-of-date, unless the subject matter is particularly topical and a special effort has therefore been made to rush the book through. Once a book is in print, as it is an expensive item to produce, publishers are in no great hurry to scrap it and replace it by a new one;

furthermore librarians do not continually throw away their old books and replace them by new – for one thing the old one might be better than the new one in some ways. This does mean that information you obtain from a book might be very out-of-date – check the date of publication on the title page.

From the point of view of how up-to-date their information is we could almost list the types of source we are discussing in an order of merit. Newspapers would be most up-to-date followed by weekly magazines; then those less frequently published (monthly, quarterly). Annual publications would come next and leaflets, booklets, pamphlets etc. next. Books would come last.

It should be remembered, however, that if the list had been compiled from the point of view of accuracy and reliability the order of merit would probably be reversed.

Libraries nowadays may also hold films, film strips, magnetic tapes, cassettes, gramophone records, and microtexts (miniature photographic copies of books, and similar material, which have to be read through a special magnifying viewer).

The librarian and his staff are valuable sources of information in themselves, always willing to answer queries or indicate to you where to find the answer for yourself.

If you get accustomed to the idea while you are at college it will stand you in good stead when you are at work – when you want to find something out, turn to a library.

12
Receiving Communication
3: Effective Reading

I. Reading more accurately

Effective reading, like effective listening, is first of all a matter of concentration and effort. Careless reading can never be effective. But a great many other factors affect your performance, most of which have to do with your general standard of intelligence and education. There is a limit therefore to how much you can hope to improve the effectiveness of your reading on a course like this. You will find, though, that the comments that follow will help to pinpoint any weaknesses you have.

Practice in reading accurately is the most valuable aid in improving your effectiveness in receiving written communication. The exercises that follow, in Section III, are designed to give you such practice – but you should supplement these by reading as much as you can on your own.

The size of your vocabulary and how accurate your idea is of what words mean are very important factors in understanding what you read. This chapter and Chapter 16 include exercises to increase your vocabulary, but again you can help yourself most of all by wide reading. What you read does not have to be of obvious educational value – reading thrillers and science fiction will also increase your vocabulary and improve your general reading ability. Reading is something you learn most about by doing it.

Your efficiency as a reader in a communication situation is also closely related to your ability to pick out quickly what is important and to summarise and remember this. This is the same sort of skill as we have just been looking at in the previous chapter. In fact note-making must be considered part of effective reading since you may often have to make notes on what you have read so that you can refresh your memory in the future without having to read through all the material again. Further practice in note-making is therefore included in the receiving practice work that follows.

II. Reading faster

It is not generally realised how much people's reading speeds vary, although you must have noticed how some students always finish first when the class is set something to read through. Most users of this book probably read at a rate lower than 200 words a minute (by 'reading', reading *and understanding* is meant – there is no point in flicking an eye quickly over a page but not grasping what is being communicated). Yet reading speeds in the region of 600 words a minute are not uncommon. Clearly the man or woman who can read at this speed is at an advantage over slower readers in a job which involves, for example, reading trade magazines and firms' technical handouts to get to know about the stock he or she is selling.

Provided you can still understand, and remember what you have read, it is worth while trying to push up your reading speed as high as you can. Spectacular increases in reading speed can only be produced by special training, but if you are rather a slow reader you can help yourself a little by taking notice of the following points.

1. *Subvocalisation*
If when you read there is a sort of silent voice in your head saying all the words you will always read rather slowly, because the silent voice cannot work much faster than you could read aloud (and that will probably not be above 200 words a minute). The 'silent voice' also wastes your energy as the muscles that you use in speaking do partially operate during 'subvocalisation' (as this process is called). It is worth while therefore trying hard to read without subvocalisation.

2. *Eye-span*
Similarly, you should struggle to avoid reading word by word. Try to grasp the meaning of several words at a time, making the group of words you take in at one time bigger and bigger as you practice. This means cutting down on the number of times your eyes move as you read a page. You can always tell a slow reader by his eye movements – the eyeballs make a continual series of tiny jerks as he goes along the lines word by word.

Quick readers may need to shift their eyes only every line and a half – or two lines – even less often. Whether you can take in a minimum of a line at a time depends somewhat on how wide the line is, of course – but it is possible by practice to widen your eye span (i.e. the width of words you can absorb without having to shift your eyes). If you get really interested in this there are books available which will help you with specially designed exercises – for example material printed with progressively more words to the line so that you can gradually widen your eye span. Such special material is outside the scope of *Oral and Written Communication* but you can have a do-it-yourself go at this sort of thing by covering up with a card all but, say, three words of a line and testing whether you can read the three words without moving your eyes. Then progress to four words and so on. A good deal of practice of this kind is necessary, however, before any lasting widening of the eye span results.

3. *Skipping*

Do not be afraid of skipping. Intelligent skipping is part of the skill of effective reading. This does not mean just casting your eye carelessly over the page, taking in a bit here and a bit there at random. It means racing through the material as fast as you can until you get to something important. Then you slow up and make a big effort to understand and remember that bit. Then you race on to the next important bit. You skip only the connecting material or what is of no importance to you.

Many people leave school convinced that there is something wrong about skipping – they seem to look on it as a kind of cheating. Some even seem to think that all fast reading is wrong and that there is some great moral value in reading everything very slowly and thoroughly. Not so. Provided you are sure you are understanding and absorbing the parts of what you are reading that matter to you, effective reading usually means reading as fast as you possibly can. And there is nothing wrong at all in leaving out altogether bits that do not seem to be telling you anything you want (or need) to know.

This is not always true, of course. You have to use your judgment. Some material – for example newspapers, magazines, novels read for entertainment only – can be read very fast with a great deal of skipping. Other material – handouts from firms, for example – can be read a little more slowly but still with skipping. Some kinds of material on the other hand – a contract or other legal document, for example – should be read very slowly and carefully in case in your enthusiasm for rapid reading you miss out some little clause that is going to turn out very expensive for you. Textbooks when you are a student usually have to be read this way too (including this one!) You are not recommended to rush the practice work that follows – you are going to be asked some pretty detailed questions about these passages.

III. Practice in receiving

Practice A
Read this passage carefully and then test your skill in receiving communication (the A questions) and making notes (C). The two B questions are there to remind you about basic points from the first part of this book.

The human body is a complex structure requiring many different foods to make it work efficiently. Firstly, like an engine, the body needs fuel which will keep it running steadily at body temperature (37° C). Fuel also to provide the running power, the energy for movement. A car engine burns petrol. The body burns food to provide energy for physical activities such as running and for the many movements of internal organs, such as breathing. Part of the food we eat must, therefore, give both heat and energy to the body. Some food is especially suited to this work because it is rich in a group of nutrients known as carbohydrates. These are of two kinds: sugars, and starches. Sugars, as you might expect, are in sweet-tasting foods—jam, honey, syrup and dried fruits. In confectionery too, such as iced cakes, boiled sweets and chocolates. Starches are chiefly found in foods made with flour, like bread, biscuits, and cakes, and all cereals like rice, macaroni and breakfast cereals. If we eat more carbohydrate food than is needed for the physical work we do, we will get fat. But fat is one way in which living things can store food for energy, so a certain amount of it is useful, and foods such as the fat from meat, butter and oily foods like herrings and nuts are all excellent providers of heat and energy for the body. Fat is the most concentrated of all the energy-giving foods.

The amount of heat or energy obtained from a food is scientifically measured in calories. Most people like foods that are rich in sugar or fats and it is these foods which have a high calorific value, that is to say they provide warmth and energy easily and to a high degree.

Patricia Searle: *Your Food*

A1. In what way is the human body like an engine?
A2. What is the principal difference between the way a car engine obtains its energy and the way the human body does?
A3. (a) Give an example of internal movement of the human body.
    (b) Is this a 'physical activity'?
A4. What two human necessities are supplied by carbohydrates?
A5. What two kinds of carbohydrate are there?
A6. How can carbohydrates make people fat?
A7. If the human body can store energy, write a sentence to say how it does it. If the human body cannot store energy, write a sentence to say so.
A8. What do calories measure?
A9. What does it mean to say that a food has a high calorific value?

B1. There are two non-sentences in this passage. Which are they?
B2. What is the topic of (*a*) the first paragraph (*b*) the second paragraph?

C. Write notes on this passage. Try not to exceed 100 words. Supply a title (not counted in the 100 words).

NOTE: You do not need to include all the examples of types of food – one example of each type will do. A good way of introducing an example in notes is to put *e.g.* in front (this means 'for example').

Practice B

The Second World War interrupted the evolution of retailing in this country. Rationing and controls of essential commodities and shortages of others meant that the distributive trades did little but distribute. Food was not just rationed; for many commodities consumers had to register with a shop, and the shop was allowed   5
just enough to supply its registered customers. There was strict price control, so that mark-ups were fixed and the element of competition was diminished. Clothes rationing put a limit on the retail side of the garment industry. All household goods, electrical equipment and furniture were in short supply and were for the   10
most part made to basic 'utility' standards. Rationing and controls, we tend to forget, continued for some years after the

end of the war. In fact, food rationing ended finally only in 1954.
The only way businesses could compete and maintain their profits
was by economising on staff, and the war made this necessary   15
anyway. 'Shop assistant' was very low on the list of essential
occupations.

This enforced economy in manpower helped set the pattern
for trading later on. The work-force in the retail industry
increased after the war, but a new way to make the industry more   20
efficient had been found. What was to take the place of workers
was really the next phase in the shopping revolution.

Greville Havenhand: *Nation of Shopkeepers*

1. Rewrite the first sentence of the passage without using the word
   evolution.
2. Give three examples each of what you would consider 'essential
   commodities' (line 2) and 'essential occupations' (lines 16 and 17) in
   wartime.
3. What is the point of the word *just* in *Food was not just rationed* (line 4)?
4. How was the element of competition diminished (lines 7 and 8)?
5. What do you think *basic 'utility' standards* (line 11) means? Why is
   utility in inverted commas?
6. Why is 'shop assistant' (line 16) in inverted commas?
7. What do you think *enforced economy in manpower* means (line 18)?
8. Rewrite the last sentence of the passage without using the words *phase*
   and *revolution*.
9. What is the difference between *evolution* (line 1) and *revolution*
   (line 22)?

Practice C

A piece of utilitarian writing should be a shop-window display
for the results of thought. A good display is never muddled or
crowded, like a side-street confectioner's shop window, choc-a-
bloc with packets, jars, boxes, tins, showcards and a somnolent
cat. A good display is simple, and it has a focal point. It is   5
therefore utterly different from a disorderly jumble, on the one
hand, and from an orderly catalogue on the other hand.

The focal point in a shop window is at eye level, near the
middle. I suggest that in utilitarian writing the corresponding
point—the most emphatic place—is the opening. It is, I believe, at   10
the opening that we must place our most important commodity—
the net result of our preparatory labours—if we possibly can.

The window of an exclusive milliner's shop contains very few
hats. Attention is concentrated on one model in the commanding
central position. A clear and flattering light and a simple,   15
unobtrusive background complete the picture. There are no
distracting details about price. Nothing can be seen of the
modiste, with her artistic eye and nimble fingers, nor of her girls

busy with production in the ribbon-bestrewn back room. The
feminine beholder, at least, has evidence enough of madame's   20
skill in her creations.

Henry Compton: Conveying Ideas

1. Which is the author's main interest in this passage – window display or
   writing?
2. Explain what purpose the subject you did not pick as the answer to the
   first question serves in the passage.
3. What is meant by (*a*) a 'flattering' light; (*b*) an 'unobtrusive' background in lines 15 and 16 of the passage?
4. What is a *modiste*?
5. What will be done in the back room (line 19)? How is it 'ribbon-
   bestrewn'?
6. What is meant by 'utilitarian' writing (line 1)? Give three examples of
   utilitarian writing.
7. Why does the author pick on a 'side street confectioner's' for the
   description of a window 'choc-a-bloc' with items. With what kind of
   shop is he contrasting it?
8. In what way is a good display different from (*a*) 'a disorderly jumble';
   (*b*) 'an orderly catalogue'?
9. In your own words say: (*a*) What sort of cat it is in the shop window. (*b*)
   What a focal point is. (*c*) What is meant by 'the net results of our
   preparatory labours'. (*d*) In what way the start of what we write is
   specially important.

Practice D

Television is the infant of the communications media; and yet, as
it exists today, it is aimed at everybody except the young, with
its bias firmly towards middle-age. There are children's programmes, and there are programmes for mature adults, and
between the two is nothing: a gap as brutal as surgery, that cuts   5
out the teens and twenties until marriage and mortgage and hire
purchase shackle the newly-weds in front of the set – to Hughie
Green and Des O'Connor, *Coronation Street* and *Callan*.*

It might be argued that pop music programmes such as *Top of
the Pops* are aimed at the young, but they are few in number, and   10
as often as not produced, directed, and even compered by
middle-aged swingers breathless in the pursuit of their long since
vanished youth. Surely this kind of programme above all others is
the one in which young people should have the greatest possible
involvement? It is, after all, the music of the young, and they   15
should be allowed to make their own case for it whether the rest
of us reject it or not.

The whole of television would seem to be somewhat ageing for
an infant; the infant already has a bald spot, and a bit of a pot on

* The author of this passage was the creator of the *Callan* TV series.

it. Its attitudes are hardening even faster than its arteries, which is   20
inevitable when you consider the people by whom it is served.
Far too many of us have been in television from its post-war
revival, and there is not nearly enough fresh, young talent coming
in.

This does not, of course, apply to actors, who accept television   25
as an essential part of their trade. The trouble is that – actors
aside – there is far too little young creative talent coming into the
medium, especially writing and directing talent, and those of us
who are older and still working in the medium are all too aware
of the fact: so we pretend. We must be the only business in   30
existence where the grown-ups pretend to be children: where a
40-year-old writer is still labelled promising: where a 37-year-old
director longing for a bowler hat and short back and sides settles
for sandals and an Afghan coat. We *need* youth in the business,
and we know it. We need it because we are aware of the dangers   35
of complacency, of familiar ground gone over until it has been
picked bare, of the comfortable illusion that what was good the
first time will be even better the hundredth.

All too often the young do not even bother to look at the box,
let alone work for it, and this is sad indeed. It has qualities of   40
immediacy and mechanical ingenuity which could and should
have great appeal to young people, and a core of mature writers,
directors and producers anxious to work with them, to share the
kind of craftmanship that takes a sizeable portion of one's life to
acquire.   45

James Mitchell in *The Daily Telegraph Magazine*

1. (*a*) When after childhood do people start again watching Television
regularly, according to the author? (*b*) Why do they start then?
2. What two reasons does the author give for not considering pop music
programmes an important contribution by Television to the entertainment of young people?
3. Express in your own words (*a*) *middle-aged swingers breathless in the
pursuit of their long vanished youth* (lines 12 and 13) (*b*) *the infant
already has a bald spot, and a bit of a pot on it* (lines 19 and 20) (*c*) *the
kind of craftsmanship that takes a sizeable portion of one's life to acquire*
(lines 43– 45).
4. In what branch of television does the author accept that there is young
talent?
5. If a '37-year-old director' really longs for 'a bowler hat and short back
and sides' what sort of person does he want to be? If he 'settles for
sandals and an Afghan coat' what sort of person does he want to *seem*?
6. Why do you think the author used the colloquialism *the box* for
television in line 39?
7. (*a*) What reasons does the author give for thinking young people ought
to want to work in television? (*b*) Why does he think they are
particularly needed?

Practice E

In a 100 years, our great grandchildren will find it appalling to imagine the river of death that runs outside our doors today. They will wonder how we could tolerate it. How *can* we tolerate it? Only because we're so used to cars that we don't notice them. But just imagine that instead of the highway, we had a high tension wire along the outside edge of every pavement, charged with enough electricity that the least contact could kill. Would we carelessly let our children run to the shop on the corner for a packet of sweets, saying 'Step carefully over the wire, dear'?

In a 100 years' time the untamed car at our doors will seem as horrible as 18th-century operations without anaesthetics do to us now.

At first the car seemed a good idea. Now it is a lethal tyrant. As Dr Mackay, of the Road Accident Research Unit at Birmingham University, points out, there are 'some 130 000 fatalities and perhaps 1 700 000 serious casualties in the western world *every* year. These figures are on the scale of a medium-sized war continuing all the time.' In Britain, the car at this moment kills four times as many people a year as the Luftwaffe did during the war years.

The car is dangerous because it is badly conceived and badly designed. Driving, considered as a task set for the computer of the brain, is just on the limit of what it can do. Driving is a great deal more demanding than flying an aeroplane, yet anyone who can read a numberplate at 25 yards and navigate slowly round the block is allowed to take several dozen horsepower out on the road; compare that with the countless precautions that are taken to train and test aircrew and the extreme vigilance imposed on the mechanical condition of their machines.

Peter Laurie in *The Sunday Times Magazine*

1. Find a word or phrase of your own that could replace the following words used in the passage: *appalling* (line 1) *tolerate* (line 3) *conceived* (line 21) *navigate* (line 25).
2. Put into your own words: *the river of death* (line 2); *the least contact could kill* (line 7); *a lethal tyrant* (line 13); *the computer of the brain* (lines 22 and 23); *the extreme vigilance imposed* (line 28).
3. What is the difference between 'fatalities' and 'serious casualties' (lines 15 and 16)?
4. How is it, according to the author, that we can tolerate 'the river of death that runs outside our doors'?
5. To what extent do you think the comparison with the high tension wire is a fair one?
6. In what sense is the car today 'untamed' (line 10)?
7. In one sentence of your own words explain why, according to the author, cars are dangerous.
8. In one sentence of your own words explain why, according to the author, people do not drive more safely.

NOTE the way the author uses numerals (lines 10, 15, 16, and 25). Many people seem to leave school with the idea that there is something wrong about numerals in written material. Of course it is slack to write *There are 3 ways of tackling this problem,* but where genuine statistical material, distances, dimensions, prices etc. are concerned, numerals are easier for the Rx to grasp than words. For precise numbers over ten, numerals are to be preferred; for approximations (*about fifty people attended*) words should be used.

Practice F

The law against deliberate or negligent debasement of food has for many years been stringent. The present Food and Drugs Act dating from 1955 follows very closely the pattern of older Acts. It is an offence to prepare to sell any food that is injurious to health; persons who are sold food 'not of the nature, substance or   5 quality demanded' can complain to their local Town Hall and have the satisfaction of seeing the retailer or manufacturer fined; it is illegal to apply a false or misleading advertisement to food; it is an offence to sell food that is not fit for human consumption.

Enforcement of the law rests with the public health depart-   10 ments of local authorities throughout the country. They have extensive powers of search and entry, they are trained in their job and they enjoy wide respect in the food and catering industry. In 1969, the latest year for which official figures exist, 1,357 shopkeepers and others were fined in England and Wales for the   15 above offences. But these were only the tip of the iceberg; the presence of a qualified and vigilant public health department in a local area – making spot checks on food premises and available to the trade for advice and discussion – is far more important than the number of summonses that actually end up in court.   20

'If you see a local retailer up before the local magistrates, you can generally reckon he has been warned or there has been some earlier trouble before – without it getting as far as the courts,' a senior inspector once told me.

But if the problem were only one of preventing deliberate   25 adulteration or faulty storage and retail habits, there would not be the considerable public anxiety about food prevailing today. Mass production methods, deep-freezing, prepackaging, artificial additives, the whole range of modern feeding stuffs, fertilisers and pesticides have created a problem that the law, despite its   30 manifest good faith and intentions, seems not wholly adequate to cope with. The law does its best. The composition of our food is rigorously controlled by complicated and detailed regulations, drafted by Ministry officials in consultation with the industry. In 1947 a Food Standards Committee was set up to advise the   35 Government on the composition, description, labelling and advertising of food. The reports of the Committee and its Food Additives and Contaminants Sub-Committee (now itself a full committee) have covered the whole range of foods, additives, and contaminants, and contained recommendations for food standards, permitted colourings and food labelling. To meet these recommendations, the Ministry of Agriculture, Fisheries and Food has brought out many new regulations and revised old ones. 40

For instance, no colouring of any kind can be used in milk. Butter must consist of not less than 80 per cent milk fat, not more than 16 per cent water and not more than 2 per cent milk solids other than fat. Processed cheese must contain differing amounts of milk, fat and water, according to the description. 45

There is still no legal standard for fish fingers. In Ireland and America, at least 60 per cent of a fish finger must be fish – but there is no official British minimum. Only in May 1969 was a minimum legal meat content laid down for sausages; 50 per cent for beef sausages and 65 per cent for pork sausages, of which four-fifths must be pork. Most European countries with equivalent food control laws would not permit the typical British 'banger'. 50

55

Fenton Bresler in *The Daily Telegraph Magazine,* June 1971

1. What is the meaning of the following words as used in this passage? *debasement* (line 1), *stringent* (line 2); *consumption* (line 9); *vigilant* (line 17), *adulteration* (line 26); *prevailing* (line 27); *rigorously* (line 33)?
2. Why are the words *not of the nature, substance or quality demanded* (lines 5 and 6) enclosed between inverted commas?
3. (*a*) What is meant by *It is an offence* in line 4? (*b*) In note form, list the three types of food that it is an offence to sell.
4. Who is responsible for seeing that the requirements of the Food and Drugs Act are carried out?
5. In what way are the 1357 'shopkeepers and others' fined in 1969 'only the tip of the iceberg'?
6. By putting the phrase in your own words show what is meant by the law's 'manifest good faith and intentions' (line 31).
7. What is the difference between *additives and contaminants* (line 38)?
8. (*a*) What permitted colouring is used in milk? (*b*) How much water is permitted in butter? (*c*) In England what percentage of a fish finger must be fish? (*d*) What percentage of a pork sausage must be pork?

Practice G

2. Subject to the Company having received from the purchaser the signed registration of user card, if any defect appears in the vehicle within a period of twelve months or within 12 000 miles usage, whichever event shall first occur, from the date upon which the goods are delivered to the first owner–user or hire-purchaser thereof, provided the goods are promptly submitted to one of the Company's authorised Distributors, the Company will repair or

replace free of all charge for labour and material any part or parts needing repair or replacement by reason of faulty material or workmanship during manufacture.

3. Any part so repaired or replaced shall be entitled to the benefit of the unexpired Warranty period or mileage; and such unexpired portions may be transferred to a second or subsequent owner provided the Company's written consent has been obtained.

4. No claims for repair or exchange will be valid unless the person claiming quotes:
   (*a*) The serial numbers of the chassis and engine.
   (*b*) The date of purchase of the vehicle and the name and address of the supplying person, firm or company.
   (*c*) Particulars of the claim, the reason therefore, and the mileage covered up to discovery of the defect.
   The Company accepts no responsibility for any parts submitted without the aforesaid information.

5. This Warranty excludes glass, tyres and batteries, the makers of which have established policies for dealing with alleged defects, and it shall not apply to normal maintenance services including but not limited to wheel tracking and balancing, brake and clutch adjustment, engine tuning, nor to components renewable under such services; e.g. sparking plugs, distributor contacts and filters.

Extract from a car warranty, Fiat (England) Ltd

For all the following questions imagine that you are the first owner of the car.

1. You have had the car ten months and completed 10 000 miles when a door stay breaks.
   (*a*) Will this be replaced under warranty?
   (*b*) Will you have to pay the labour costs?

2. If you had had the car thirteen months but completed only 10 000 miles when the stay broke would that change the situation? If so, how?

3. If you had had the car only ten months but completed 14 000 miles what would the situation under warranty then be?

4. How many separate items of information must you supply when making a claim under warranty, over and above the model number of the car and your name and address? You are not required to list these items, only to count them.

5. Why is no warranty given by the company against tyre failure?

6. (*a*) Does the warranty consider wheel balancing a part of normal maintenance?
   (*b*) Can wheel balancing be adjusted under warranty under any circumstances?

7. If you sell the car to somebody else is he automatically protected by this warranty?

8. If a part is replaced under warranty what guarantee of the replacement part is given by this warranty?

9. If you are entitled to repair or replacement of a faulty part under warranty, (*a*) can you take the car to any garage of your choice for this to be carried out? (*b*) must you return the car to the firm that you bought it from?

10. You bought the car on 1 April (i.e. you paid the money for it on that date). At that time you had a leg injury that made it impossible to drive a car so the firm agreed to drive the car to your house for you. They did this on 3 April. You were not able to drive the car yourself until 14 April. From what date does your twelve months warranty start?

Practice H

The following chart based on information supplied by the Central Office of Information indicates changes in consumer spending between 1960 and 1970.

| | *Per cent of total spending* | |
	1960	1970
Food (household expenditure)	25	20.5
Alcoholic drink	5.5	7
Tobacco	6.5	5.5
Housing (rent, rates, etc.)	10	12.5
Fuel and light	4.5	5
Clothing and footwear	10	8.5
Cars and motor cycles	3.5	3
Other durable goods	5	4
Running costs of motor vehicles	2.5	5.5
Other travel expenditure	3.5	3
Catering (meals and accommodation)	5.5	5
Other goods	9.5	9.5
Other services	9	11
	100	100
Total value of consumers' spending *at current prices*	£16 933m.	£31 238m.
Total value of consumers' spending *at constant 1963 prices*	£18 445m.	£23 396m.

1. What is meant by *consumer spending*?
2. Why is it necessary to add *household expenditure* after the entry *Food*?
3. What is meant by *Other durable goods*? Give three examples
4. Give three examples of *Other goods*.
5. Give three examples of *Other services*.

6. Why is it useful to show the total value of spending at *constant 1963 prices* as well as *current prices*?

7. Write a paragraph of about 100 words indicating the change of pattern in consumer spending that occurred during the ten years for which information is provided.

Practice I

Just as few adolescents can ever believe that their parents have been through the same stages of attitude and development before them, so one of the more frequently recurrent fallacies has been people's belief that their own age is without precedent, that some new order is coming to birth in which all the general   5
assumptions previously made about human behaviour are becoming somehow outmoded. In few ages has this belief been more prevalent than our own.

In fact there were few ingredients in the bubble of excitement which welled up in the years after 1956 which have not in essence   10
appeared in various guises in many other societies and times. To take the most obvious example, the 'revolt of youth' against tradition and their elders has been a repeated theme, as we can see from that much-quoted remark by a thirteenth century monk: 'The world is passing through troublous times. The young   15
people of today think of nothing but themselves. They have no reverence for parents or old age. They are impatient of all restraint. They talk as if they alone know everything'. Again, widespread immorality and promiscuity are hardly innovations of the twentieth century, even when elevated into some new moral   20
system. It is hard to believe that Juvenal was not writing of D. H. Lawrence and the intellectual enthusiasts for *Lady Chatterley's Lover* when he decried: 'High flown moral discourse from that clique in Rome, who affect ancestral peasant virtues as a front for their lechery.'   25

However 'modern' any attitude may seem, counterparts can generally be found in many other ages. Even that phenomenon which we so particularly associate with our own time, the division of society into the 'with-it' and the 'squares', is hardly unfamiliar. We find the same language used: the term 'square', for instance,   30
in its contemporary sense, was a coinage of the 1770s, when it was used to describe those who still affected square-toed shoes after they had gone out of fashion; and in the plays of Thomas Otway, written in seventeenth century Restoration London, we find the words 'swinging' and 'swinger' used exactly as they are   35
used today, to denote the lively, 'swinging' handful who recognised no conventional moral restraint, and were in revolt against the boring majority who did not know what life was about.

Christopher Brooker: *The Neophiliacs*

1. What do the following words mean, as used in the passage?
   assumptions (line 6); *prevalent* (line 8), *promiscuity* (line 19); *elevated* (line 20); *decried* (line 23); *clique* (line 24); *counterpart* (line 26); *phenomenon* (line 27); *contemporary* (line 31); *coinage* (line 31); *denote* (line 36)
2. In your own words, what is it that the author says most adolescents cannot believe about their parents?
3. If something is a 'recurrent fallacy' what two things do you know about it?
4. What would be remarkable about an age 'without precedent'?
5. If assumptions about human behaviour are becoming somehow 'outmoded' what has happened to them?
6. (*a*) What other word does *guises* (line 11) remind you of?
   (*b*) What does 'have not in essence appeared in various guises' mean?
7. If widespread immorality and promiscuity are 'hardly innovations of the twentieth century' what do we know about them?
8. (*a*) What word makes it look as if the author used an American translation of Juvenal?
   (*b*) What does the word mean?
9. In your own words, what is the author's view of a swinger?
10. Write notes on this passage. Try not to use more than 100 words. Give your notes a title (not counted in the 100 words).

13
Communicating by Telephone

Although – by the use of such appliances as the Remotecopier – we can now send by telephone pictures, graphs, drawings, replicas of documents etc., the telephone is still fundamentally a device for transmitting spoken words over a distance. Using the telephone is therefore a special kind of oral communication but one that, although very convenient, does present communication problems not present when we are speaking to the Rx face-to-face. If we are to use it to the best effect we have to be aware of these difficulties and try to compensate for them.

I. Advantages and disadvantages of telephoning

The principal advantages of direct oral communication may be briefly listed as:

1. Speed of transmission (e.g. no delay while message is being delivered).
2. Proof of transmission (the Tx knows he has delivered his message; with written material it is virtually impossible to be sure the Rx has read the message, and difficult to be sure it has even reached him).
3. Speed of feedback.
4. Ease of correction (mistakes can be rectified as soon as noticed; adjustment of message as a result of feedback can be immediate).
5. Use of non-verbal supporting media (i.e. tone of voice, gestures, facial expressions etc.).

The principal disadvantages of direct oral communication are:

1. The Rx has only one chance to receive the message (he cannot study it later at leisure except by means of notes taken at the time).
2. No detailed record of what the Tx said (this has important legal implications).
3. The Tx has to think his ideas out as he transmits them and choose his words quickly as he talks with no chance to revise them.
4. It can only be used where the distance between Tx and Rx is very short.

Communication by telephone has all the disadvantages of direct oral communication except the last. It also has all the advantages except the last – but that is a very important exception.

Some tone-of-voice modification of the words used is possible over the telephone, but this often does not come through as clearly as the Tx expects. A jokey or teasing manner, for example, often fails completely over the telephone because of this, and the Rx can be seriously offended by a dry remark that face-to-face (when he could identify the tone of voice used more accurately) he would have laughed at. You have, therefore, to pick your words particularly carefully when you are on the telephone and work very hard at sounding friendly and helpful.

The loss of gesture and facial expression is a serious deprivation that those who use the telephone a good deal have to train themselves to allow for. It is quite difficult if you are inexperienced in telephone communication to remember, for example, that the Rx cannot see that you are smiling. Much of the advantage also of speed of feedback is neutralised by the fact that the Tx cannot read feedback on the Rx's face as in direct oral communication.

Since the Rx has not got you to look at, he concentrates on your voice to a degree never reached in face-to-face talk. To some extent this is useful – he really is *listening* to you, and not *watching* you. But this concentration does also mean that he notices every slip that you make – little grammatical errors, the wrong word used, mispronunciations etc. – in a way that he would not if he was in front of you. He also notices much more clearly anything unusual about your voice – for example, a lisp, or regional or class accent, or a foreign accent. This is why it is that somebody whose Lancashire accent (for example) you had previously hardly noticed suddenly sounds like a Lancashire comedian when he phones you up. His voice has not changed and the telephone has not distorted it – it is just that without his facial expressions to watch you give much more attention to the sound of his voice.

You can see that a number of factors militate against completely satisfactory communication when you are on the telephone. If you are the one initiating the call there is a further point to think about – timing. With written communication the Rx can (more or less) choose when he will read your message. With face-to-face oral communication you usually take some trouble to pick the best time to raise the point you want to discuss. Often you ask the Rx if it is a convenient time to speak to him. Over the telephone, however, you force yourself upon him at a time chosen to suit you, not him. He is almost certain to be disturbed by your call when he is doing something else. You need to be particularly polite and tactful to make up for this.

II. Good telephone practice

SPEAKING DISTINCTLY

1. Hold the receiver so that the mouthpiece is about an inch from your lips.

2. Speak slowly and clearly. Remember to sound the consonants of your words. Do not shout.
3. If you have difficulty in making the person at the other end understand you, do not allow signs of irritation or embarrassment to show. Try to increase clarity by pausing slightly between words. If you are a man, raise the pitch of your voice; if you are a girl, lower it.
4. For special clarity with words spelled out use the Post Office telephone alphabet (see Appendix 2). For numbers that cause confusion (such as *16, 60*) count up to them (viz. *thirteen, fourteen, fifteen, sixteen,* with a slight emphasis on the final number).

INITIATING A CALL

1. Know what you are going to say before you start. Unless it is very short and simple, have a few notes in front of you.
2. Be polite. Remember, you may be phoning at a very inconvenient moment.
3. A few friendly social remarks at the beginning and end of a business call – if you know your Rx a little – lubricate the machinery of communication. It is easy to overdo this, however, and waste your Rx's time with chatter which he finds it difficult to bring to an end.

ANSWERING A CALL

1. Announce yourself or your firm immediately. It used to be the recommended practice to say your number but this wastes time as the caller then usually has to ask who is speaking. The standard procedure if you are a junior is to say, for example: 'Jackson & Spearings', when you pick up the telephone. It is pleasant to add: 'Good morning' or 'Good afternoon', Some people like also to hear: 'Can I help you?' Only the first of these three is essential but the other two certainly add an air of friendly helpfulness. Never just say: 'Hello'. Even more maddening is the person who just says: 'Yes?'. If you are on an extension it can be assumed your operator has given the firm's name and you should, on picking up the phone, give the name of your department (sometimes, your name). If it is necessary to give your name (and this is always the case with private calls) the formal method for men is to use the surname only, in such phrases as: 'Thompson here' or 'Thompson speaking'. Ladies add *Miss* or *Mrs* and usually say something like: 'This is Miss Thompson'. It is best to be formal even when answering private calls until you know who is at the other end.
2. Listen actively. Make notes if necessary. Ask for names and unusual words to be spelled out.
3. Try to avoid transferring a call. Do your best to deal with the caller yourself – it is very irritating to be transferred from person to person and have to repeat your business every time.

If you do have to transfer a caller to another extension let him know what you are doing. If there is delay, keep in touch by such comments as: 'I am still trying to connect you'. Do everything you can to avoid the position where the caller is left listening to an extension phone ringing that it is quite clear nobody is going to answer – he has no way of getting back to you or your exchange and has to ring off and start again. The call may have been an expensive one or one he had waited half the morning to place.

4. If the caller asks for somebody unobtainable and you are unable to give him any satisfaction yourself, ask if he will (*a*) ring later; (*b*) be rung later; (*c*) speak to somebody else; (*d*) leave a message. In such a case it is important to make a clear note either of the message (many firms have special telephone message pads) or of what is to be done. Be sure the caller's name, address, and telephone number are accurately written down. Make sure the message goes to the person it concerns with minimum delay.

COMMUNICATION POINTS

1. Remember the disadvantages in using the telephone already mentioned. Work hard with your tone of voice to make up for the loss of facial expression. Choose your words very carefully. Try to avoid slips of the tongue, pronunciation errors etc.
2. Avoid colloquialisms such as *OK* and *Hang on*. Many people dislike these on the telephone and think a firm whose employees use them slack.
3. Treat the telephone not as an inanimate object but as something living. There is a live human being at the other end, remember.

For discussion

For convenience, in any of the following questions where reference to a 'boss' is necessary (i.e. the head of the firm if it is a small concern, the head of the section you work in if it is a big concern) he is assumed to be called 'Mr Brown'.

1. You have a very junior job with Codd, Haddock & Co., Wholesale Fish Merchants. If you have to answer the telephone what should you say on picking up the phone?
2. You are an important enough person with Codd, Haddock & Co. to have your own extension telephone. What should you say each time you pick up your phone?
3. You are serving at the counter singlehanded and several customers are waiting. You can hear the telephone ringing in the back of the shop and nobody seems to be there to answer. What should you do?
4. You answer the telephone at 9.20 a.m. and the caller asks for Mr Brown. You know Mr Brown is away for the morning but will be back in the afternoon. What should you say to the caller?
5. You answer the telephone to a long-distance caller who wants Mr Brown. You know Mr Brown is out in the yard checking in a consignment of goods. It will take you three or four minutes to get him to the telephone. What should you do?

6. You have your own extension telephone. A call has been put through to you by the firm's operator but after a few moments it becomes clear that the caller should really be talking to Mr Brown. (*a*) What should you say to the caller? (*b*) What should you do?

7. The caller asks to speak to Mr Brown. You know that Mr Brown is tied up for several days with visits to retailers that you supply and is making only brief and irregular appearances at the warehouse. What is the best procedure and what should you say to the caller?

8. The basic situation is as in the previous question but the caller (*a*) stresses that what he has to say is urgent and important and (*b*) refuses to speak to anybody but Mr Brown. What is the best procedure and what should you say to the caller?

9. You answer the telephone and the caller immediately starts on a long and complicated series of complaints. These have nothing to do with you personally and the caller is so angry and excited that you find it very difficult to make much sense of what he is saying. What is the best procedure and what should you say to the caller?

10. What is wrong with the following telephone dialogue? How would you allocate the blame between the two speakers?

Answerer: Codd, Haddock & Co. Good morning.

Caller: I want to complain to somebody. That last lot of fish I had from you yesterday was in a disgusting condition. I shan't be able to sell any of the plaice – it's stinking. I'm keeping it for you to look at.

Answerer: I am very sorry you are dissatisfied, sir. Actually, this sort of thing isn't my job I'm afraid. The person you really want is Mr Brown. He's out on a visit at the moment but I'll get him to call you the moment he gets back.

Caller: Well there's not much point in prolonging this call if you're not the person responsible, I suppose. But make sure your Mr Brown gets on to me immediately. I want him to see that fish today.

Answerer: I understand sir. Rest assured I shall get Mr Brown in touch with you as soon as he comes in. He'll either phone you or come right round. Goodbye (*hangs up*).

14
Writing More Ambitious Sentences

For discussion
The following pairs of versions of the same material all differ in the same way. What way? For each pair decide which version you prefer and why. Did you come to the same conclusions each time? Consider in detail how each (*b*) version has been changed from its (*a*) version.

1(*a*) These marketing figures have been compiled by a well-known research organisation. They will probably surprise most supermarket managers. The research organisation has been operating in the grocery field for many years.

1(*b*) These marketing figures, which have been compiled by a well-known research organisation that has been operating in the grocery field for many years, will probably surprise many supermarket managers.

2(*a*) Agriculture yields the whole of the food consumed in the world. Exceptions to this are the comparatively small products of fishing, hunting, and collecting. Agriculture also provides a considerable part of the raw materials of industry. The most important are cotton, wool, and flax.

2(*b*) If we except the comparatively small products of fishing, hunting, and collecting, agriculture yields the whole of the food consumed in the world while also providing a considerable part of the raw materials of industry of which the most important are cotton, wool, and flax.

3(*a*) The history of transport is one of gradually improving efficiency. Man has slowly increased his control over machines. He has obtained a greater return in work for the same input of energy. Such progress has been very uneven. In some parts of the world the most primitive methods are still in use.

3(*b*) The history of transport is one of gradually improving efficiency as man has slowly increased his control over machines, obtaining a greater return in work for the same input of energy, but such progress has been very uneven so that in some parts of the world the most primitive methods are still in use.

As you become more experienced and confident in writing you will grow more ambitious and will want to use longer and more complicated sentences. The discussion you have just been engaged in will have revealed that many people find them pleasanter to read than a series of short ones. On the other hand, it is a mistake to think that long sentences are automatically better than short. Very long sentences are, in fact, a handicap to good communication. American research has shown that sentences over twenty words in length strain the less educated Rx's ability to grasp what he reads and there is no reason to think things are much different in the U.K.

It is true, though, that command over longer sentences enables us to add variety to our sentence structures and to give a professional finish to our writing. The danger is that in trying to increase sentence length you may just jam sentences together and thus slip back into the kind of sentence error (wrong sentence division) dealt with in Chapter 7, section IV.

This chapter aims to show you how to write sound longer sentences.

There are a number of recognised ways by which two or more sentences can be *linked* together (as distinct from being *jammed* together) to form new longer sentences. The most useful of these are described in the subsections that follow, along with some warnings about particular pitfalls associated with their use.

Always remember, though, that you can link together successfully only such sentences as already belong together in sense. Otherwise you will offend against what is known as 'unity of the sentence'. A sentence must be felt by the Rx to deal with only one topic. Thus the sentence *The professor answered all the questions in the quiz without difficulty and fell down stairs on his way out of the studio* is unsatisfactory because although soundly *constructed* it breaks the rule of unity by trying to deal with two quite separate pieces of information at once.

1. Linking by conjunction

The words most commonly used as conjunctions are: *after, although, and, as, because, but, for, how, if, since, so, than, that, though, unless, until, when, where, whether, while, why.*

> He was in a hurry to nail up the crate. He hit his thumb with the hammer. Because he was in a hurry to nail up the crate, he hit his thumb with the hammer.

NOTE: Rather surprisingly, conjunction links do not always have to come between the two sentences linked.

The following special points about conjunction linking should be remembered.

1. You will have been told at school not to use *and* too often as a link. This is not merely because *and* is the commonest link and the Rx tires of it. *And* is a completely neutral link; it adds no meaning. Compare *Because he was in a hurry to nail up the crate, he hit his thumb with the*

hammer with *He was in a hurry to nail up the crate and hit his thumb with the hammer. And* does not show the connection between the sentences linked as *because* does. We sometimes want a neutral link – then *and* is perfect; but when there is a logical connection between the parts joined which can be indicated by selecting the appropriate conjunction, using *and* wastes an opportunity to help the Rx.

2. *Also* is not a conjunction.
   NOT *He did not take sufficient care in nailing up the crate, also he hit his thumb with the hammer.*

It should too, as a general rule, be avoided as the first word of a sentence (i.e. the sentence above is still unsatisfactory even if a full stop or semicolon is put after *crate*).

3. *Therefore* is hardly ever completely satisfactory as a conjunction. *He did not take sufficient care in nailing up the crate; therefore the goods fell out in transit* is much less clumsy than *He did not take sufficient care in nailing up the crate, therefore the goods fell out in transit. He did not take suffcent care in nailing up the crate, so the goods fell out in transit* is smoother than either.

4. There is some disagreement about the use of *so* as a conjunction. With the sense of 'therefore' – as in the sentence in 3 above – it seems perfectly satisfactory. With the sense 'in order to' it is better to follow it with *that* than to use it alone – *He nailed the crate down hurriedly so that he would not be late stopping work.* With the sense 'also' it is not satisfactory as a conjunction.
   NOT *He left on time that day, so did Jackson.*
   BUT *He left on time that day as did Jackson.*
   OR *He left on time that day; so did Jackson.*

5. *Like* is regularly used as a conjunction in America. This usage is spreading in the United Kingdom (especially in speech) but is not yet generally accepted. At the moment it should not be so used in formal writing.
   NOT *Please leave the storeroom like you found it.*
   BUT *Please leave the storeroom as you found it.*

2. Linking by participle

He was in a hurry to finish the job. He nailed the crate down with insufficient care.
Being in a hurry to finish the job, he nailed the crate down with insufficient care.

The sentences above illustrate the use of the present participle (the part of the verb ending in *ing*) as a linking device. It is particularly useful when the actions of the two sentences joined take place at the same time (i.e. it is at the same time that he is in a hurry that he is nailing down the crate).

Where the action of one sentence takes place *before* the action of the other, linking can be neatly achieved by the use of *past* participles (such as *opened, gone, been* etc – the *ed* ending is usual):

> *The goods were despatched by road the same day. They were received earlier than the customer had expected.*
> *Despatched by road the same day, the goods were received earlier than expected by the customer.*

Having plus a past participle is a very useful form of this kind of linking:

> *The assistant checked that the gloves had not been damaged. He then changed them for a larger size.*
> *Having checked that the gloves had not been damaged, the assistant changed them for a larger size.*

Notice how participle linking saves words – the linked version is usually one or two words shorter.

A special point to watch out for in using participle linking is to make sure that the participle makes sense with the noun or pronoun that is the subject of the sentence, because the Rx will *expect* this to be the noun or pronoun to which the participle refers.

Thus NOT *Despatched by road the same day, the customer received the goods earlier than expected* because it is not the customer who was despatched by road. *Despatched* in this sentence is what we call an 'unrelated participle' – i.e. it is not properly related to any word in the sentence.

Similarly NOT *Having checked that the gloves had not been damaged they were changed for a larger size,* because *they* (the pronoun standing for the *gloves*) does not make sense with *having checked* (gloves cannot check gloves).

3. Linking by relative pronoun

The principal relative pronouns are: *who, whom, whose* (for persons); *which* (for things) *that* (for either) *where* (for places) *when* (for times). The following sentences illustrate their use as links:

> *The assistant refused to change the gloves. They had been damaged.*
> *The assistant refused to change the gloves, which had been damaged.*
> *That is the man. He attempted to leave the shop without paying, last Tuesday.*
> *That is the man who attempted to leave the shop without paying, last Tuesday.*
> *That is the man. I saw him take the necklace from the jewellery counter.*
> *That is the man whom I saw take the necklace from the jewellery counter.*
> *That is the man. His umbrella was left in the shop.*
> *That is the man whose umbrella was left in the shop.*

The noun that the relative pronoun refers back to in the sentence (e.g. *gloves* in the first example, *man* in the other three) is called the 'antecedent'. You should take care when using relative pronoun linking to keep the antecedent and the relative pronoun next to each other (as in the examples above). Where other words including a noun come between the antecedent and the relative pronoun the Rx becomes confused; he is uncertain which noun *is* the antecedent. An example of this sort of confusion is the sentence *I am writing in reply to your letter of 15 May about your umbrella which has been unfortunately overlooked for some weeks.* 'Is it the umbrella or the letter that has been overlooked?' the Rx wonders.

A relative pronoun must *have* an antecedent. A common error is to use a relative pronoun where there is no antecedent for it to refer back to (the antecedent exists only in the Tx's mind, not in the sentence). Thus *He had failed to reply to this letter for almost six weeks which was very remiss of him* is unsatisfactory as it supplies no antecedent for *which*. It would have been better to keep this as two sentences: *He had failed to reply to this letter for almost six weeks. This was very remiss of him.*

Exercise 26
Using what you have learned so far, link the following groups of sentences in the neatest way you can that gives good sense. (Do not use *and* or *but*.)

1. He ran all the way from the bus to college. He was ten minutes late for class.
2. He opened the envelope with a table knife. He cut his hand.
3. The student had to work all day Sunday to catch up with his homework. He had done no homework the previous week.
4. Mr Tompkins is our representative in your area. He will call on you to discuss your complaint.
5. The student passed his examinations. He was promoted.
6. The assistant phoned the office before 5 p.m. He was unable to stop the letter. It had already been posted.
7. The customer was very aggressive in her attitude. She annoyed the sales assistant. The assistant was less helpful than he might have been as a result.
8. The customer was unable to produce a receipt. The sales assistant refused to change the gloves. They were quite clearly defective.
9. He did not check the consignment in detail. He signed for fifty tins of paint which had not been delivered. They appeared on the delivery note.
10. Students in employment used to work all day every day and study in the evenings. They had no leisure time except at weekends. This was in the days before day-release.

Before we go on to further sentence exercises it is important to realise that the way we are now looking at sentence linking is just to help you build your sentences better. Experienced writers do not start off with two or three sentences and then find a way of linking them – they link them straight away.

Furthermore it is often possible to find satisfactory short cuts. For example, suppose we wanted to link the two sentences: *The professor was a very learned man. He answered all the questions in the quiz without difficulty.* We might decide that relative pronoun linking was best and write: *The professor, who was a very learned man, answered all the questions in the quiz without difficulty.* However, if we were to write instead: *The professor, a very learned man, answered all the questions in the quiz without difficulty* we achieve the same result with fewer words – we seem to get the effect of relative pronoun linking without actually putting the relative pronoun in (or the verb that follows it). In this version, by the way, the words *a very learned man* are said to be 'in apposition'. They repeat the subject in different words. In fact, with this particular example, we could go further in streamlining our sentence and write: *The learned professor answered all the questions in the quiz without difficulty.*

NOTE the commas round (a) *who was a very learned man,* and (b) *a very learned man.* It is particularly important to use these commas correctly when you use relative clauses (i.e. groups of words including a verb and introduced by a relative pronoun) like (*a*) above.

If the relative clause merely *describes or adds information* about its antecedent *it must be enclosed between commas.* If it *defines* the antecedent *it must not be enclosed between commas.*

COMPARE: The professor, who was a very learned man, answered all the questions in the quiz without difficulty (descriptive) WITH: *The professor who had a large wart on his nose answered all the questions in the quiz without difficulty* (defining). Here *who had a large wart on his nose* is used to indicate, or define, which of several professors we are talking about.

If we wrote: *The professor, who had a large wart on his nose, answered all the questions in the quiz without difficulty* we would make the clause descriptive again and we would be back with only one professor to think about. Now the wart on the nose is not mentioned to pick him out from a group but just as a piece of descriptive detail, a little extra that the reader might like to learn. The commas make all that much difference.

NOTE. We cannot use *that* to introduce a descriptive relative clause, only a defining one. *The professor that had a wart on his nose answered all the questions in the quiz without difficulty* defines which professor we are talking about and it is impossible to have a descriptive version with commas round *that had a wart on his nose.* Clearly it would be much easier for everbody if we always used *that* to introduce defining clauses and *who, whom,* and *whose* for descriptive clauses, thus avoiding relying on the commas. But language is not like that – nobody can make a whole nation change its language habits overnight. It is the custom to use *who, whom,* and *whose* for both defining and descriptive clauses, indicating the difference by commas – and it will stay that way for a very long time to come.

Exercise 27

Which of the following contain defining clauses that do not need commas? Which contain descriptive clauses that must have commas round them? Which could be punctuated either way, with a shift of sense according to whether the commas are there or not?

(*a*) Words which are spoken in anger are often regretted afterwards.
(*b*) My sister who is a very good cook makes wonderful sausage rolls.
(*c*) The sister who went to cookery classes at the college is a very good cook but the elder girl can hardly boil an egg.
(*d*) The drawer in which the money had been kept had been broken open.
(*e*) The usherette who had a torch showed him to his seat.
(*f*) Students who check words they are uncertain of in a dictionary before they write them down seldom make spelling errors in their homework.

Exercise 28
Sentence linking exercises move one stage nearer the real-life situation when you have to pick for yourself what sentences *can* be joined.

Improve the following paragraphs by linking sentences in any way which seems to you appropriate.

(*a*) Early man took to drawing on walls and scratching on pieces of bone. He began with pictures of animals and hunting scenes. This is not surprising. They were very important in his daily life. Many cave paintings have lasted from the Stone Age to the present day. They are still visible. They have the original colour on them. They were done on walls deep inside the caves. They were beyond the limit where daylight could penetrate. It is hard to believe they could ever have been painted. The conditions would have been difficult. There could have been only a feeble artificial light. It would have come from crude stone lamps. They would have used animal fat as fuel.
(*b*) Jewels are personal adornments. Some items may originally have been useful. They may have been symbols of rank. They may have been seals. Many races of people have made jewellery. They have lavished care and craftmanship on them. We have knowledge of ancient jewellery. It comes from three sources. In the first place there are pictures or representations of jewels. These were carved. They were sometimes painted on pottery. Next are genuine pieces. These have been unearthed. They are rare. Then there is funeral jewellery. This comes from tombs. The pieces are often very fragile. They seem to be token items. They are made of the thinnest metal. Sometimes, even, the stones are imitation.
(*c*) Kew Gardens is a popular name. It stands for the Royal Botanic Gardens. It covers 288 acres. These are by the river Thames near Richmond. This town is in Surrey, England. It is now virtually part of London. People go for pleasure. They see the beautiful gardens. There is another side to the subject. The real aim is to study plant life. New plants have been introduced into Britain. They have been introduced by botanists from Kew. Plants have been successfully transferred. They have been transplanted from one part of the world to another. Rubber was brought from South America. It was skilfully transferred to Malaya. It is not easy to transplant rubber. Cinchona was introduced into India. This is another South American plant. Its bark is used to produce quinine. This is a drug used against malaria. This is a

dangerous illness. There are other possibilities. These may include introducing plants into Africa. They could include transferring plants from Africa.

Exercise 29

Criticise and improve the following sentences. All the faults are ones mentioned in this chapter.

(*a*) Having been late six times in the first fortnight of his employment, the manager told the new assistant that he would have to go.

(*b*) Jones is the name of the assistant who I passed the order to.

(*c*) You have not been able to produce any documentary evidence that you bought these goods at this store, therefore I am unable to exchange them or refund your purchase money.

(*d*) I checked all the items against the delivery note also entered them afterwards in my Receipts book.

(*e*) These items were entered on the advice note and were not amongst the goods delivered on 1st May.

(*f*) Customers will not put up for ever with check-out queuing, travelling on buses, and searching for bargains, which waste their time.

(*g*) Entering the store from Rosebery Road the cigarette counter is the first selling area encountered.

(*h*) Lizards and snakes are slaughtered for the sake of their skins that are made into shoes and handbags.

(*i*) Most mothers today are not confined to their homes like their own mothers perhaps were.

(*j*) He passed all the invoices for payment without checking them which is typical of his generally negligent attitude.

15
Avoiding Ambiguity

I. The dangers of ambiguity

By 'ambiguity' we mean that the medium of communication has been used in such a way that more than one interpretation is possible. The Rx is then uncertain which meaning is intended or – worse – sees only one of the possible meanings and that not the one intended by the Tx. Many of the examples given in this chapter are quite amusing; but this must not disguise that ambiguity can lead to serious, even disastrous, misunderstanding. Our first example may have caused the death of two men.

One November evening in 1952 two teenagers – Christopher Craig, aged 16, and Derek Bentley, 19 – were on a warehouse roof in Croydon with the intention of robbing it. They were detected and it was not long before the police arrived on the roof. Bentley was arrested without a struggle but Craig had a gun. According to the evidence given at the subsequent trial by the police officer who arrested Bentley (and by other officers on the scene) Bentley shouted 'Let him have it, Chris!'. Immediately afterwards Craig started firing and a policeman was killed – those words hanged Bentley.

At the trial it seems to have been accepted that the words were a direct incitement to Craig to fire on the police officer who had arrested Bentley and – although in fact it was not that officer who was killed – Bentley was sentenced to death. To this day argument continues about whether this was the true interpretation of what he meant. The words he used were ambiguous; perhaps not only the police but Craig himself misunderstood them. Bentley had not resisted arrest, had allowed a knife to be taken from his pocket, and had handed over the knuckleduster that was his only other weapon. Could his words have been intended to mean something like: *Hand over your gun to the police officer, Chris*?*

Verbal communication, especially in English, seems particularly prone to ambiguity, but it can occur in other media.

* This defence was not used at the trial because the defendants denied that the words had ever been used. Bentley was of very low intelligence level and unable to read or write.

Here is a reproduction of a photograph of the heat control on a widely used room heater. It comes from the user leaflet intended to show purchasers how to use this control, but some have found it confusing. Do the arrows indicate which way to turn the knob to lower (or raise) the heat? Or do they indicate which numbers represent reduced heat and which increased heat?

Figure 5 consists of two ambiguous drawings. Drawing A is seen about equally by people at first glance as representing either a man's face or a long-haired girl kneeling. They have little difficulty in seeing the second interpretation once it is pointed out to them. Drawing B is more baffling. Some people at first sight see this as portraying an attractive (though old-fashionedly dressed) girl; others as revealing a hideous old hag. In this case, however, most people have considerable difficulty detecting the opposite interpretation from the one they first fix on. (If you need a couple of clues – the left eye of the hag is the left ear of the girl; the cruel mouth of the hag is the black band round the neck of the girl.) This is the great danger of ambiguity in using words too – the Rx when he first reads your words or hears you speak may fix on a meaning quite unlike the one you intend and be unable to free himself from this and thus continue to misinterpret you. Unfortunately we often do not realise the Rx has misunderstood us and are therefore unable to put the matter right. It is necessary therefore always to check our words for ambiguity.

We usually think of ambiguity as a mistake – something that occurred by accident. This is not always so. The two drawings in Figure 5 were obviously drawn that way deliberately. Words are frequently used with intentional ambiguity.

Figure 5

In Shakespeare's *Antony and Cleopatra* Antony, on the eve of his critical battle with Octavius Caesar, asks his lieutenant, Enobarbus, how he will fight next day. Enorbarbus replies: *I'll strike, and cry 'Take all'*. Antony is delighted with this reply, assuming that Enorbarbus means that he will strike many blows at the enemy and make them take all the punishment he will dish out. But Enobarbus's reply is deliberately ambiguous – his private meaning is that he will strike his colours (i.e. surrender) and tell the enemy to take all his arms and equipment.

Similarly, some advertising copy is deliberately ambiguous. *Artificial silk* is frequently abbreviated to *art. silk* in small ads. Surprisingly often the full stop to mark the abbreviation is omitted; many innocents then believe that the scarf or tie on offer is made of real silk of a specially artistic kind. A *leather grained briefcase* may seem to a casual reader to be made of leather. Not every Rx notices the second meaning – that the unspecified material of the briefcase is surfaced with a leather-like graining finish. Even the term *post free*, so often included in advertising copy, has frequently an element of deliberate ambiguity. It does not very often mean that the firm supplying the goods is meeting the cost of postage. It usually means that postage has been included in the price – the customer is still paying it.

Sometimes the ambiguity of our language is exploited by advertisers, not to deceive but to attract attention. The advertisement on page 114 is an example. This sort of use of ambiguity is harmless enough, but illustrates how ambiguous our language can be.

You have to watch out for ambiguity both as Rx and as Tx.

As an Rx you must try your best to make sure that you have taken the Tx's communication in the sense intended. You should be particularly careful to watch out for any deliberate ambiguity in the wording of advertisements, sales literature, contracts etc.

As a Tx you should check to make sure that what you write or speak has only one meaning.

Sometimes the second meaning is so ludicrous that the Rx is not likely to have any serious doubt what is intended – for example: *Mrs Johnstone poured the tea while Mrs Smithers carried in the cups*, or *If the baby does not thrive on fresh milk, boil it*. Such sentences are, of course, not so completely useless as ones like *The assistant told the buyer that he had been late four times that week*, where there is real doubt what is being said. They are nevertheless to be avoided, because while the Rx is smiling at the unsuspected second meaning he is not concentrating fully on what he is being told and communication is that much less effective. Besides, nobody wants to be laughed at when he is not trying to be funny.

Again, some examples of ambiguity leave the Rx in no real doubt what his response is supposed to be, but irritate him vaguely because they seem to say two things at once. In a train lavatory there appears a somewhat mysterious statement:

GENTLEMEN
LIFT THE SEAT

Is this an order – all gentlemen are commanded to lift the seat? Or is it a statement – it is a characteristic of gentlemen that they lift the seat. Are British Rail ordering men using the lavatory to lift the seat? Or are they gently coaxing them to do so by assuming they will all want to be considered gentlemen? This kind of ambiguity is also to be avoided.

Group activity
A. Search through any magazines or newspapers you have at home and try to produce at least one example of each of the following:

1. An ambiguity in an advertisement which you think is deliberate and intended to deceive the potential customer. (You will be rather lucky to find one of these as they are, fortunately, not common.)
2. A deliberate ambiguity intended to attract attention to an advertisement.
3. An accidental ambiguity in a headline (these occur frequently as a result of having to force a great deal of meaning into a very small number of words).

B. Compare your finds in class and try to work out for each the cause of the ambiguity.

II. Causes of ambiguity

If you carried out the group activity at the end of the previous section with some enthusiasm you probably managed to detect the principal causes of ambiguity for yourselves.

The most obvious cause of trouble is words which have more than one meaning. This usually produces rather bizarre second meanings as: *Miss*

Pickhill grasped the pince-nez which hung from a sort of button on her spare bosom* or

TUBE TRAIN ON FIRE
PASSENGERS ALIGHT

Some of the most baffling ambiguities arise when we use pronouns and the Rx is uncertain which noun already used is being replaced by the pronoun. This is the trouble with *The buyer told the assistant that he had been late four times that week.* Does *he* refer to the assistant or the buyer?

If you think again about Bentley's alleged words on the warehouse roof you will see that the ambiguity is essentially of this kind, being caused by uncertainty as to what was meant by *it.*

We are sometimes told that pronouns should always refer to the last noun mentioned – but this does not seem to help much in reducing ambiguity. If we take the sentence *The sales assistant unpacked the gloves from their boxes and threw them in the waste-paper bin,* although boxes *is* the last noun mentioned most people immediately think of the sales assistant throwing the gloves away (i.e. they take *them* as referring to *gloves* not *boxes*).

Every time you use *he, she, it, they, them* etc. you should check that the Rx can be in no doubt about which noun the pronoun is replacing. We often start a sentence with *This* or *That* referring back to the preceeding sentence – here too you must check to make sure that the Rx has no doubt what noun in the preceeding sentence is being referred to.

Faulty word order can produce a special type of ambiguity where strictly speaking the meaning that common sense tells us was *not* intended by the Tx is the only one the sentence has. We are supposed to put next to each other in our sentences ideas that we want the Rx to associate together. If therefore we write *In the early seventies trouser suits were still being produced for women on a large scale* it could be argued that the sentence is not ambiguous at all – it refers to large-scale women and that is the end of it! Certain words have to be placed particularly accurately in the sentence if ambiguity is to be avoided. *Hardly, almost, only, scarcely, generally, usually* are the commonest trouble-makers. In one theatre – which had better remain nameless – there is a sign which reads:

BEER IS SERVED IN THE UPPER CIRCLE BAR ONLY DURING THE INTERVALS

What does that mean? No beer in the upper circle bar before the performance starts? Or no beer in the stalls and circle bars during the intervals? How can the *only* be shifted to give one or other of these meanings instead of both at once?

Word order has a considerable effect on meaning. What difference would it have made if four sentences back the author had written: *No beer before the performance starts in the upper circle bar*?

---

* Quoted in *Fowler's Modern English Usage* (2nd edition) which has a very interesting section on ambiguity for those who would like to follow the subject up in more detail. There will almost certainly be a copy in your library.

For discussion

1. Look at the sentence: *The buyer told the assistant that he had been late four times that week and he would have to report this to the manager.*

How many meanings can you find in this? Which do you think the most likely to have been intended? How would you reword it to give that meaning?

2. In their book *Reader over Your Shoulder* Robert Graves and Alan Hodge tell the story of a local council that erected a sign outside the park reading:

NO DOGS MUST BE BROUGHT TO THIS PARK EXCEPT ON A LEAD

It was objected that this meant that even if you did not take the dog inside it had to be on a lead when you brought it to the park gates.

The Council then put up a second sign:

DOGS ARE NOT ALLOWED IN THIS PARK WITHOUT LEADS

This was objected to on the grounds that it was directed at the dogs rather than the owners, and dogs cannot read.

(Incidentally, there is a notice at the entrance to the cattle-market in a certain Sussex town which reads ALL PIGS TO THE RIGHT.)

The council had a lively session on this notice and the following notices were in turn proposed, and in turn rejected:

(*a*) *Owners of dogs are not allowed in this park unless they keep them on leads*
(*b*) *Nobody without his dog on a lead is allowed in this park*
(*c*) *Dogs must be led in the park*
(*d*) *All dogs must be kept on leads in this park*

What objection can you see to each of these? Make suggestions for rephrasing the notice; criticise your own suggestions; decide on the most satisfactory solution.

Exercise 30

Point out any ambiguity in the following. Rewrite to make clear the meaning you believe to have been intended.

(*a*) I found a dead sparrow digging in the garden.
(*b*) Every time I raise my finger I want you to break a small piece off.
(*c*) He drew his chair closer to the fire for it was never warm in the evenings.
(*d*) I can recommend the applicant for the position he is applying for with complete confidence.
(*e*) Nobody has worked at this branch for two years.
(*f*) When did you arrange to check the stock?
(*g*) We have received an order from the Parks Superintendent at Blenkinsop for 6000 red and yellow tulips.
(*h*) LONGHAIRED SCHOOLBOY SUSPENDED BY HEAD

(*i*) I am not recommending this tape recorder because it is a discontinued model that is being sold off cheaply.

(*j*) We received your letter this morning and I assure you we shall waste no time in dealing with your complaints.

Exercise 31

Comment on the cause of ambiguity in each of the following and rewrite to avoid it.

(*a*) (Plumber's bill)
To taking up board to look for smell and replacing same – £1.20.

(*b*) (Letter to a Borough Surveyor)
Could we please have permission to put a porch over the back door which faces north and makes the kitchen very cold. John . . . will do it for us as he has a glass top and wooden bottom that will fit.

(*c*) (Headline *Liverpool Echo*)
MAN HELPS MURDER POLICE

(*d*) (Notice in greengrocer's window)
BRUISED GRANNIES 8P PER POUND

(*e*) (Sales notice)
STYLISH LADIES' COATS

(*f*) (House agent's advertisement)
Rooms to let in best part of North London, suitable for two young ladies, fifteen feet long by twelve feet wide.

(*g*) (Heading to advertisement)
THIS PROJECTOR ENLARGES SNAPSHOTS, PHOTOS, STAMPS – EVEN LIVE INSECTS UP TO 10 FEET HIGH – IN FULL COLOUR!

(*h*) (From a newspaper report of a cricket match)
Richards was almost brilliantly caught by Barwell at slip when 16, but thereafter the cover drives flowed and the issue was quickly settled in the 23rd over.

(*i*) (Card in a shop window)
BARMAID NEEDED FIVE EVENINGS A WEEK. MUST BE THOROUGHLY EXPERIENCED OR USELESS.

(*j*) (Notice in a tailor's shop)
SUITS MEASURED IN YOUR HOME. ALL AREAS COVERED.

(*k*) (On a pillar-box in Lagos)
POST NO BILLS

Exercise 32

The following notes were given to the author as directions for finding a college of further education by car from the town centre. It was known how to start off, as the supplier of the note had pointed this out, but several subsequent points of difficulty were discovered.

2nd right – traffic lights
1st left – one mile
x roads – college right.

(*a*) Point out the ambiguities in this note.
(*b*) Rewrite the note to avoid these.
(*c*) Rewrite in sentences as directions given in letter.
(*d*) Write out these directions as if given orally, avoiding all ambiguity.

16
Picking Your Words

I. Word power

Word power is simply a matter of the size of your working vocabulary. Your working vocabulary consists of those words that you have completely at your command (i.e. you know what they mean; can pronounce and spell them; can use them with confidence in speech and writing.) People's working vocabularies vary enormously in size. It has been estimated that many men whose employment never rises above the simplest manual jobs manage all their lives on a working vocabulary of fewer than 4000 words. A university professor, on the other hand, may have ten times this number of words at his command. Samplings carried out by the author indicate that students from hairdressing and retailing normally have vocabularies in the 8000 – 15 000 range, the majority falling into the 10 000 – 12 000 bracket. Ten to twelve thousand words do not seem very many to cope with all the communication problems of work and private life.

Since words are the basis of spoken and written communication it is obvious that increasing the size of your vocabulary must have a favourable effect on your ability to communicate; but the good effect is not so automatic as you might think. We have all come across people who seem to know a great many long words but cannot communicate. When you are the Rx the gain is absolute – the more words you know the better you will understand what you hear and read. When you are the Tx (and that is the role we are considering in this chapter) the advantages are more limited. You may know words that the Rx does not know – such words are useless to you for communicating with that particular Rx. And there is much more to communicating than having a big vocabulary. Nevertheless, it is clearly an advantage to have a lot to choose from when you are picking your words.

Vocabulary exercises of the sort that come later in this chapter may slightly increase your total vocabulary, but are more useful for sharpening your understanding of words that you already have a vague knowledge of and bringing these up into your normal working vocabulary. Some people find browsing through a dictionary and learning new words at random interesting and useful, although it does seem a most unnatural activity. By far the most satisfactory method of increasing your vocabulary is by reading and listening. This means especially reading, and listening to, material that you find rather difficult in vocabulary and whenever you meet an unfamiliar word looking it up in a dictionary or asking somebody about it.

II. Exactness and suitability for the Rx

From the communication viewpoint the two questions that really matter in choosing our words are:

1. Does the word mean exactly what we mean (exactness)?
2. Is it the right word for the Rx (suitability for the Rx)?

EXACTNESS

In all communication we must use words exactly, but for the kind of work students using this book are engaged in it is often extra important, because there is a legal obligation under the Trade Descriptions Act of 1968 to be exact. Is the statuette we are selling a *copy* of the one in the British Museum? Or is it a *duplicate*; a *replica*; a *reproduction*; an *imitation*? Is this a *wool* sweater or a *woollen* sweater? Is is a *pure wool* sweater? In the restaurant – a *duckling* is not the same thing as a *duck*, a *peach melba* is not just a peach with ice-cream (it must include melba sauce, which should be made from raspberries). The hotel receptionist cannot describe as a *suite of rooms* two rooms and a bathroom that are separate. The hairdresser has to be careful what she describes as a *rinse*, what as a *dye*, and so on. Should a raincoat be described as *waterproof,* or *showerproof,* or *shower resistant,* or *weatherproof*?

SUITABILITY FOR THE RX

Picking an exact word will not solve any communication problem if it is a word the Rx does not know. If the customer asks the waiter, 'What fish is the "fried fillet of fish" on the menu?' and the waiter replies, with complete accuracy, *'Gadus morrhua'**, it is most unlikely that any communication will have taken place at all.

If we are interested in communicating we cannot afford to ignore the Rx. We cannot choose words that we think he may not know (we have to be particularly careful here with technical terms pertaining to our trade). We also cannot choose words that may shock or annoy him, or give him an unfavourable opinion of us or the establishment we work for.

This means, sometimes, making a very quick assessment indeed of the educational standing and likely vocabulary size of our Rx (based often on no more than the first few words he speaks to us) while at the same time trying to form a lightning impression of the kind of person he is. This is, of course, a very difficult task and one where we are unlikely to get 100 per cent correct answers very often. But we should try. And be prepared to

* Cod.

make adjustments if we find our first estimate of the Rx was wrong. Above all we should not choose our words to please ourselves; to show how clever we are or how big our vocabulary is. We should always be prepared to speak (and write) very simply indeed if this is necessary to ensure that the Rx completely understands us. This is what communication is about – seeing it from the other person's point of view not our own.

All this assumes an Rx whose educational standard and vocabulary size is below our own. Of course, very frequently sales assistants, hairdressers etc. are dealing with customers whose educational standard and vocabulary size is above theirs. In such cases they can only do their best to hold their own and hope that the customer knows a little about communication principles and is trying to suit his/her vocabulary to theirs.

III. Synonyms

When we are picking our words, as described in the preceding section, we are making a selection from a number of words all very similar in meaning. Such words are called 'synonyms'. It should be noted that synonyms are nearly always words *similar* in meaning; they are rarely *identical* in meaning. Few words are identical in sense with each other (*furze, gorse, whin* are examples of this rare condition – the three words are fully interchangeable). Generally speaking it is precisely because they are *not* fully interchangeable that synonyms have stayed a part of the language – there is not much point in having two words that do exactly the same job. As it is, the tiny differences permit us to pick one word (from several) that has just the shade of meaning we require – provided we know all the synonyms available and the differences between them. *Copy, duplicate, replica, reproduction, imitation,* in the preceding section, provide a good example of synonyms with tiny shades of meaning difference separating them. (What are they?)

Sometimes synonyms are to be distinguished from each other not so much by meaning as by 'tone'. Some words are more poetic than others; some more dignified; some sound rather comic and can be used only in lighthearted material; some are unemotional, others emotional; some have a scientific or technical tone etc. Along with the two main factors in selecting our words, we also try to match the tone of the words to the circumstances – we use different words in business from those we use at home; different words when we write from when we speak; different words in a formal situation from those in an informal situation, and so on.

For discussion
A. What sort of difference is there between the synonyms that make up the following pairs: *seller, vendor; purchase, buy; lonely, solitary; tranquil, calm; spectacles, glasses; monstrosity, freak; swindle, fraud; elliptical, oval; vanquish, defeat; map-making, cartography; merchandise, goods; textile, woven?*

B. What differences in meaning can you detect between the synonyms in the following groups? (NOTE: It is a meaning difference if one of two synonyms indicates a stronger, or more intense, degree of the other; thus *hot* differs from *warm* by degree.) Do any of the synonyms seem identical to you in both meaning and tone and therefore completely interchangeable?

1. *need, want*
2. *dear, expensive, costly*
3. *excess, surplus, increase*
4. *eradicate, exterminate, eliminate, destroy*
5. *fault, error, defect, flaw*
6. *genuine, pure, real, authentic*
7. *blame, censure, upbraid, reprove*
8. *deface, disfigure, mar, injure*
9. *old, ancient, antiquated, obsolete, antique*
10. *rude, insolent, impolite, abusive, offensive*

IV. Areas of meaning

The words we use are symbols – they stand for ideas in our minds. The Tx can, for example, use the word *book* to represent the kind of object you are now reading these words in. We transmit these symbols to the Rx and he replaces the symbols by ideas in his own mind. If both Rx and Tx have used the symbols correctly the same idea should appear in the Rx's mind as started in the Tx's. When the Rx reads, or hears, the word *book* he knows – approximately – the kind of object the Tx is referring to. For this system to work at all successfully the following conditions must be observed.

1. The Tx must use standard symbols that everybody accepts. If you decide to name what everybody else calls a 'book' a *bront* you will not get very far in communicating about books. This means that you have to know the standard uses of all the words you employ.
2. The Rx must know the word the Tx uses (as we noted in section II) and must have an accurate idea of its recognised meanings. If, for example, like surprisingly many people, the Rx thinks that *livid* stands for either 'red-faced' or 'angry' (instead of 'lead-coloured') there will be some misunderstanding when he reads a phrase such as 'the livid face of the corpse'.

All this would be a great deal more foolproof if we had only one symbol for each idea, and one meaning for each symbol – but, of course, language is not like that. We have just noted in the preceding section that we frequently have more than one symbol for the same idea, or much the same idea (synonyms). We also have to recognise that the one symbol may have several meanings – or, more exactly, areas of meaning. For example if you were to say just the word *book* to a group of twenty people, twenty different ideas would form in their heads. Each idea of a book would be different in size, shape, colour, binding, contents etc. Nevertheless, everybody would probably be within the same area of meaning. If somebody thought of *book* as 'making a reservation' that would have brought in a different area of meaning. *Book* in the sense of 'a large-scale composition in words' is a different area of meaning from *book*, the physical object consisting of a collection of printed sheets bound together. A *book* as a division of a larger work (e.g. *the books of the Bible*) should probably also be recognised as a separate area of meaning. And what about the *book* that the racing man thinks of first?

You will see that when a word is used in isolation there may be doubt as to which area of meaning is intended. Even if the word has only one area of meaning there will be doubt about the precise shade of meaning. *Lawn-mower* has only one area of meaning – but there is a great deal of variation possible within that one area. It is, of course, unnatural to use words in isolation like this; we normally use words in sentences and the rest of the sentence helps us to make the meaning clear. You will see that it is a mistake to believe that there is one 'correct' meaning for every word. If even a simple everyday word like *book* can prove to have several meanings it is no wonder that people argue and disagree so much when they use abstract words like *fair, cheap, reliable* etc. where there is no physical object to be pointed out to settle an argument (as there is with at least the best known area of meaning for *book*).

For discussion
1. How many areas of meaning can you find for the following words: *train, lace, pitch, staff, counter, suite*?
2. (*a*) What do you consider to be the meaning of: *fair, cheap, reliable. martyr, wire, art*?
   (*b*) What have you learned from this discussion?
3. (*a*) How far is it possible to distinguish between the following garments: *pullover, slipover, jersey, club jacket, cardigan, sweater, jumper*?
   (*b*) Between *ale* and *beer*?
   (*c*) Between *inn, hotel, hostelry, public-house, pub, guest house*?
4. We are able to talk about a *landlady* as well as a *landlord*, a *headmistress* as well as a *headmaster* but we do not seem to meet the following:
   bakeress, charman, chairwoman, airhost, watchwoman, forewoman, ton-up girls, she-woman.
   Why is this? (The answer may not be the same for each word.)
5. With each of the following words, which sex do you think of immediately? Why?
   doctor, nurse, teacher, principal, barrister, sales assistant, customer, workmate, neighbour, boss.

V. Confusing words

When two words look or sound rather similar the Tx sometimes mixes them up and uses the wrong one. This sort of confusion can make the Tx look silly, as when a schoolmate told the author's son, 'We always have two holidays in our family because we are effluent'. The Rx can, of course, make the same mistake (i.e. the Tx uses the right word but the Rx gives it the meaning of a similar sounding word.) This sort of error is called 'malapropism' after the character Mrs Malaprop in the eighteenth-century play *The Rivals* who specialises in such verbal mixups as calling another character 'the very pineapple of politeness' (instead of *pinnacle*).

A second common cause of confusion is when two words are pronounced alike but spelled differently (for example, *die* and *dye*). We have a considerable number of puns of this kind in English and people do tend to become uncertain which word is which.

"I suppose you could call us birds of pray"

For discussion

A. How do you distinguish between the words in the following pairs, all of which are common causes of malapropism?

affect, effect	defective, deficient
alternate, alternative	disinterested, uninterested
amend, emend	ensure, insure
biannual, biennial	exhausting, exhaustive
censor, censure	impracticable, impractical
consist of, consist in	judicious, judicial
credible, creditable	lightening, lightning

luxurious, luxuriant
official, officious
permissible, permissive
physical, psychical

precede, proceed
septic, sceptic
statute, stature
stimulus, stimulant

B. Make sure you know how to distinguish between the words in the following pairs with identical, or almost identical, pronunciation.

always, all ways
anyone, any one
assent, ascent
brakes, breaks
boy, buoy
broach, brooch
bow, bough
canvas, canvass
check, cheque
council, counsel
core, corps
cubical, cubicle
currant, current
draft, draught
dyed, died
every day, everyday
faint, feint
flair, flare
flea, flee
flour, flower
formerly, formally
hair, hare

herd, heard
hoard, horde
key, quay
led, lead
licence, license
meat, meet
meter, metre
passed, past
pier, peer
plane, plain
practice, practise
president, precedent
principal, principle
rain, reign
rough, ruff
sew, sow
sheer, shear
stationery, stationary
sty, stye
tale, tail
troop, troupe
throes, throws

C. Are you sure you know the difference between

it's and its;
there, their, and they're;
to, too, and two?

VI. The uses of dictionaries

Dictionaries are very useful for checking the spelling of words but that is far from their only use. A dictionary's first job is to tell you what words usually mean – i.e. it is the principal way that Tx and Rx ensure that they are using their symbols in the same way. All but the smallest dictionaries will also tell you some, or all, of the following:

1. How the word is pronounced.
2. What 'part of speech' it can be (i.e. verb, noun, adjective etc).
3. What the plural is of a noun if this is unusual; what the past of a verb is, if irregular etc.
4. What the origin of the word is.

A good dictionary will aim to show all areas of meaning, not just the most obvious one. The largest dictionaries may even include a few phrases to show how the word is used.

It is clear that all this information cannot be given in a small cheap dictionary and you are strongly recommended to buy for your personal use as good a one as you can afford. After all, you will be making use of it all your life.

Certain dictionaries have great authority – partly because they have been compiled on sound research lines and are not just taken from other dictionaries, but also because they are known to be those most frequently consulted. The Oxford dictionaries (there is a whole range of them) come into this category along with Webster's *International* (American) and Chambers's *Twentieth Century*. Good buys for your personal use, as they are fairly small and not too dear, are the *'Pocket' Oxford* (which requires rather an outsize pocket) and the *'Little' Oxford* (very much smaller but including less information, of course). You can back up your fairly small personal dictionary, if necessary, by reference to the big expensive dictionaries in your college library and the public reference library.

DICTIONARY CHASES

1. Check how good your dictionary is by seeing how many areas of meaning it shows for the following words: *air, bar, cannon, gill, gorge, stock.*
2. Check the meaning and pronunciation of the following words, which are not at all uncommon: *geriatrics, ghetto, gibberish, gillie, gingham, glaucoma, glissando, glockenspiel, gossamer, goulash.*
3. Check the following words, which are really rather uncommon – and there are hundreds more just as unusual, without going outside the letter *g*. (You will probably need to turn to the big library dictionaries for these.) *Gerah, gesso, ghee, gimmal, gimp, ginkgo, girandole, glabrous, gnomon, greywacke.*
4. Check the pronunciation of: *amateur, chaos, formidable, lieutenant, macédoine, pâté, reservoir, schedule, schooner, vase.*

For discussion
The following letter from a reader was published recently by *The Daily Telegraph*. What points could be made in reply?

SIR – To open a jar of well-known English crab pâté, one is advised to 'pry off' the lid. My dictionary definition of the verb 'to pry' gives 'to look curiously; to peer; to nose about'. There must surely be an easier way to open a jar of pâté?

Exercise 33

A. People
1. Looks on the bright side   *o* . . . .
2. Looks on the dark side   *p* . . . .
3. Uses his wealth or skill for the good of
   mankind   *p* . . . .

4. Contemptuous of the aims and beliefs of
   others   c . . . .
5. Thinks about his own good only and
   enjoys talking about himself   e . . . . . .
6. Devotes himself to others and does not
   seek reward for doing so   a . . . .
7. Has an irresistible tendency to steal   k . . . .
8. Has special skill in judging art, music,
   wine and food etc.   c . . . .
9. Hates women   m . . . .
10. Devoted to the pleasures of eating and
    drinking   e . . . . . .

B. *Places*
   1. Where birds are kept   a . . . . .
   2. Where bees are kept   a . . . . .
   3. Where fishes are kept   a . . . .
   4. Where medicines are compounded   d . . . .
   5. Where animals are slaughtered for the
      market   a . . . .
   6. Where refuse is burned to ashes   i . . . .
   7. Where water is collected and stored   r . . . .
   8. Where money is coined   m . . .
   9. Where grain is stored   g . . . . . .
   10. Where goods are stored   d . . . .

C. *Trades and professions*
   1. Tests eyesight and sells glasses   o . . . .
   2. Treats diseases of the eye   o . . . . . .
   3. Compounds and, legally, sells drugs and
      medicines   p . . . .
   4. Cares for feet   c . . . .
   5. Sets up printing type   c . . . .
   6. Draws plans, engineering diagrams etc   d . . . .
   7. Sells fruit, vegetables etc from a barrow   c . . . .
   8. Deals in furs   f . . . . . .
   9. Deals in wines   v . . . . . .
   10. Loads and unloads ships   s . . . .

D. *Sciences and skills*
   1. Effective speaking   e . . . .
   2. Cultivating and management of gardens   h . . . .
   3. Study of ancient buildings and
      prehistoric remains   a . . . .
   4. Study of coins   n . . . .
   5. Making fireworks   p . . . .
   6. Study of mankind   a . . . .
   7. Study of the varieties of human race   e . . . .
   8. Study of the working of the human body   p . . . .
   9. Study of the working of the human mind   p . . . .
   10. Study of birds (feathered kind)   o . . . .

E. Miscellaneous

1. Consisting of several kinds   *m* . . . .
2. Exclusive right to sell a commodity   *m* . . . .
3. Unable to pay your debts   *i* . . . .
4. Word for word   *v* . . . .
5. Fluent in two languages   *b* . . . .
6. Reduce to powder   *p* . . . .
7. Capable of being reduced to powder   *f* . . . . . .
8. Wasteful in spending   *e* . . . .
9. Capable of being drawn out (of metals etc.)   *m* . . . .
             or   *d* . . . . . .
10. Easily broken   *f* . . . . . .
11. A paid job with no duties   *s* . . . .
12. An addition to a will   *c* . . . . . .
13. Loss of memory   *a* . . . . . .
14. Flesh-eating   *c* . . . .
15. Vegetation-eating   *h* . . . .
16. Eating all kinds of food   *o* . . . .
17. The white of an egg   *a* . . . . . .
18. Able to adapt to many situations   *v* . . . .
19. To compensate for loss or damage   *i* . . . .
20. The space left unfilled in a cask or bottle before it is sealed   *u* . . . . .

Exercise 34

1. For each of the following sets of words (*A*, *B*, and *C*) write down the lefthand column and place beside each word a synonym selected from the righthand column.
2. What differences (if any) can you detect between the synonyms you have thus paired up?
3. What have the words in set *A* in common that makes them different from set *B*?
4. In what way is set *C* different from both the other sets?

A		*B*	
perplexity	accuracy	abbreviate	elicit
vocation	disclosure	inaugurate	estimate
revelation	accomplishment	convey	gyrate
craftsman	facsimile	determine	prophesy
opulence	affluence	assess	expedite
copy	vitality	rotate	transport
feat	bewilderment	heighten	introduce
energy	termination	predict	signify
conclusion	artisan	accelerate	elevate
precision	occupation	indicate	condense

C

pliant	*effective*
principal	*graceful*
vigilant	*uncouth*
rigid	*able*
obsolete	*antique*
crude	*firm*
serviceable	*equivalent*
elegant	*main*
capable	*supple*
synonymous	*wary*

Exercise 35
Study the following passage and answer the questions which follow:

An examination of our newspapers shows that the great majority of them are extraordinarily uniform with regard to what news is included, what omitted, and what comments are made. On those occasions when newspapers of rival political views take up strongly opposed sides there is *very seldom* any discussion of the views of the other side. Few newspapers report the opinions of foreigners about British policy, unless that opinion *happens* to be favourable. There are honourable exceptions, but those newspapers are not *widely read*. The lack of variety is not, on reflection, surprising. I was at first surprised when I began to study different newspapers. This was so because I had not reflected upon the fact that most of the newspapers with the biggest circulations are owned by a *comparatively* small group of men. Sixteen London newspapers (ten daily papers and six Sunday papers) are *owned* by five groups of proprietors.

Susan Stebbing: *Thinking to Some Purpose*

1. Give *one* word from the passage which means the same as:

   (a) *study*
   (b) *friendly*
   (c) *meditation*
   (d) *sales*
   (e) *owners*

2. Give *one* word which could be used in the passage in place of:

   (a) *very seldom*
   (b) *happens*
   (c) *widely read*
   (d) *comparatively*
   (e) *owned*

3. Explain *in your own words* five ways in which the treatment of news by the great majority of newspapers is similar.

(Union of Educational Institutions)

17
Putting in the Punctuation

I. Commonsense about punctuation

People who are not very skilful at communicating in writing often excuse themselves by some such comment as: 'I'm afraid I've never been much good at punctuation.' It is as if they admit to this to avoid admitting what they should really confess – which is: 'I cannot put what I want to say clearly into words. I am not able to write in sentences. I cannot write my own language properly.'

Punctuation is not nearly so important a part of writing as it is made out to be. Punctuation will not make up for weak sentence structure, illogical order of ideas, inaccurate choice of word, failure to think of the Rx – in short, punctuation will not put right what is wrong to start with. On the other hand, incorrect punctuation can make otherwise sound writing ambiguous or difficult to understand.

Punctuation is an aid to the Rx. It is there to show him how the sentences are constructed, how he is to read them. Just sufficient punctuation to do this is all that is needed. More confusion is caused by unnecessary punctuation marks than by punctuation marks omitted, and the modern tendency is towards shorter sentences and minimum punctuation.

The brief guide to the use of the various marks of punctuation that follows tells you the basic rules. You will be well advised not to put in any punctuation that you cannot justify by one of these rules.

II. Full stops

A. The full stop is used to mark the end of a sentence. A common mistake is to substitute a comma for the full stop. This goes deeper than a mere punctuation error – it reveals a faulty idea of what a sentence is. We discussed this at length in Chapter 7.

B. The full stop is also used to indicate *abbreviations*. Two systems are generally used. You should choose one and keep to it.

System 1. All abbreviations are followed by a full stop (e.g. *Esq.* for Esquire and *Mr.* for Mister). This is the older system and the more widely used.

System 2. A distinction is made between abbreviations which consist of the first part of the word abbreviated only (*Esq.*) and those which leave out the middle of the word and therefore end with the letter that the full word ends with. In this system the second type of abbreviation does not take the full stop (*Mr*). This is the system used in this book. It is a little more logical, and slightly reduces typing time.

Abbreviations which consist of the initial letters of a group of words are usually shown with full stops by those who use System 1 (*B.B.C*; *m.p.h.*) and without full stops by advocates of System 2 (*BBC*; *mph*).

There has been a marked tendency over the last thirty years or so to choose names for institutions, inventions etc. that permit the abbreviated form to be pronounced as a word e.g. REME – Royal Electrical and Mechanical Engineers (one of the earliest examples); ERNIE – Electronic Random Number Indicating Equipment; laser – light amplification by stimulated emission of radiation.

Abbreviations of this pronounceable kind are called 'acronyms'. The letters that make up an acronym never have full stops after them.

For discussion
How many acronyms can you think of? What words do the initial letters stand for?

III. Commas

Commas are used to separate parts of a sentence that would be confusing to the Rx if they all ran into each other. Here are some examples of the most common application of commas.

A. To separate the individual words or items making up a series of three or more.
Example 1: *For meat, cheese, butter, bacon, frozen vegetables there are reach-in refrigerator cabinets in self-service stores.*

NOTE. Five items, four commas to separate them. You would normally expect to use one comma fewer than the number of words or items to be separated.

Example 2: *The thieves made off in a long, grey, high-powered car.*

NOTE. Three words describing the car, two commas to separate them. If only two words had been used a separating comma would not have been required:

Example 3: *The thieves made off in a long grey car.*

If the last item of a series is joined on to the others by an *and* it is still correct to put the comma in. (People seem to pick up at school the quaint idea that you must never put a comma in front of an *and*.) In Example 1 there could well have been an *and* in front of *frozen vegetables*. This would not have changed the punctuation.

B. To separate phrases or clauses making up a series of three or more.

'Phrases' are groups of words going together in sense (such as *out of doors, down the street*). 'Clauses' include a verb and are usually the result of sentence linking (e.g. two sentences linked together by conjunctions produce one sentence of two clauses).

Example 4: *During a shopping expedition to a large departmental store a woman may wish to get her hair set, cash a cheque, have a meal, as well as just make purchases.* (Phrases separated.)

Example 5: *Students must obtain their own entry forms, check that their qualifications for entry satisfy the regulations, and see that they pay their entry fees before the closing date for applications.* (Clauses separated.)

NOTE. Most people would consider the comma before *and* in this sentence optional.

C. To separate an introductory word, phrase, or clause from the main part of the sentence.

Example 6: *However, no one store can supply all these requirements.* (Introductory word.)

Example 7: *When tins and packets are thrown higgledy piggledy into a basket, more are sold than would be from a carefully assembled stack.* (Introductory clause.)

D. By enclosing it between two commas, to separate a word, phrase or clause from the rest of a sentence that would still make complete sense without the material thus enclosed.

Example 8: *Shopping in a department store is made pleasant by the comfortable, even luxurious, conditions provided.*

Example 9: *William Whiteley, who built up a huge store in London, boasted that he could supply anything from a flea to an elephant.*

Example 9 should have reminded you of that part of Chapter 14 where we discussed the difference between descriptive clauses (enclosed between commas) and defining clauses (never enclosed between commas).

For comparison here is a sentence with a defining clause introduced by *who* (and therefore with no commas enclosing it).

Example 10: *A young woman who buys a new suit at a department store can see and buy many matching accessories.*

Exercise 36

Explain the difference in meaning between the following sentences.

1. (*a*) The principal stores involved in this takeover bid are Jacksons, Spearmans, Fields, Richards and Jones, and Tomlins.
   (*b*) The principal stores involved in this takeover bid are Jacksons, Spearmans, Fields, Richards, and Jones and Tomlins.
2. (*a*) The shop which was converted to self-service last year has shown a substantial increase in turnover during the past six months.
   (*b*) The shop, which was converted to self-service last year, has shown a substantial increase in turnover during the past six months.
3. (*a*) However, he arranged the tins of corned beef. They looked very unattractive.
   (*b*) However he arranged the tins of corned beef, they looked very unattractive.
4. (*a*) Rather unwisely, he decided, the manager would authorise a full refund in such cases.
   (*b*) Rather unwisely, he decided the manager would authorise a full refund in such cases.
5. (*a*) As we have now recovered the original keys for this cabinet, we are returning the replacements sent by you with your invoice.
   (*b*) As we have now recovered the original keys for this cabinet, we are returning the replacements sent by you, with your invoice.

Exercise 37

To be punctuated correctly the following passage requires only full stops and commas. Where should these come?

Self-service shops cut a shopkeeper's expenses assistants freed from the work of serving customers are needed only to take money at the checkouts or to cut weigh label and pack goods for restocking shelves with their lower running costs self-service shops can attract extra customers by reducing prices on the other hand some people do not like self-service shopping in particular old people despite all the signs find that searching for goods is tiring without doubt the success of self-service shops shows that they are popular with many customers particularly young housewives who appreciate the additional speed shopping time is often cut down by a half a boon to customers with young children it seems certain that unless the shopping habits of the nation change very considerably the expansion of self-service shops and supermarkets at the expense of the conventional shops especially in the grocery trade is inevitable.

IV. Dashes (–)

Full stops and commas are by far the most widely used and important punctuation marks. Probably the next most useful is the dash. This will be a surprise to those who left school believing that dashes were not proper punctuation marks at all. This common (and completely mistaken) idea probably arises from the desperate attempts of teachers to prevent pupils from (wrongly) using dashes instead of commas and full stops. In fact, the dash has three important jobs to do and – in the right circumstances – it can do each of them better than any other punctuation mark.

Use 1. The last sentence demonstrates this. Two dashes can be used to enclose material 'in parenthesis', a word or phrase or clause inserted into a sentence which would be complete (though less detailed or less exact) in sense without it. We have just seen in the previous section that a pair of commas is frequently used to mark off a 'parenthesis', although we did not then use this word. Another method is by brackets (see the last sentence but one – and what you are reading at this moment is also a parenthesis in brackets).

Why do we have three ways of doing the same thing and how does the dash fit in? Personal taste comes into this a good deal and it is not possible to give fixed rules, but brackets provide the heaviest insulation from the rest of the sentence and commas the lightest. When we jump away from our main sentence to add some additional point of interest not all that closely connected and then come back to the main sentence again we generally enclose the additional information between brackets. If the parenthesis is very closely connected to the main sentence in sense we use commas. For the many parentheses* that we feel fall somewhere between the two we use dashes. Again, if there are already several commas in a sentence we may prefer dashes to commas to enclose the parenthesis so that the parenthesis stands out well. The example that follows illustrates both commas and dashes used to mark parentheses in the same sentence.

Example 1: *She would be, he estimated, twenty-six or twenty-seven years old, although her singularly inept hair style – plaits coiled into round pads over her ears – gave a first impression of mid-thirties.*

Use 2. A dash is very useful in sentences which start with a subject consisting of a number of items in series. The Rx becomes worried reading a very long series of subjects and begins to wonder what has happened to the predicate. A dash followed by a word such as *these, those, all* in front of the predicate helps the Rx to grasp the sentence.

Example 2: *Meat, cheese, butter, bacon, frozen vegetables – all can be stored in reach-in refrigerator cabinets in self-service stores.*

Do not, by the way, confuse dashes with hyphens, of which there are two in this example. Hyphens join words together to form compound words (*reach-in, self-service*). In handwriting and printing (but not in typed material) they are made a little shorter than dashes to assist the Rx to distinguish them.

Use 3. The dash is particularly useful to show a break of continuity in a sentence. For dialogue in novels etc. it is the usual way of indicating that somebody has started to say something but does not finish. More important – it can be used in any form of writing to indicate that the sentence has a break in it after which it either (*a*) goes on in another

---

* Note this plural.

direction perhaps to a surprising ending, or (*b*) is completed by words that the part of the sentence before the break has had the Rx waiting for.

Example 3(*a*): *He rushed to place a chair for this important-looking customer – and tripped over her umbrella.*

Example 3(*b*): *A young woman who buys a new suit at a department store can see and buy many matching accessories – gloves, handbag, shoes, umbrella, scarf, even jewellery and lipstick.*

(*NOTE* also the use of the commas in this sentence – *jewellery and lipstick* are thought of as a second series, following *even,* and as there are only two items no comma is used before the *and*.)

For discussion
What do you consider to be the best way of punctuating the following?
(*a*) How students are taught is and always has been far more important than what they are taught.
(*b*) One year of teacher training is quite inadequate particularly for the teacher of very young children where teaching skills are of special importance.
(*c*) We consider this a new and not unwelcome technique for increasing sales at the smaller branches.
(*d*) As at present organised the body of teachers within a technical college are divided into departments between which there is little contact concerning the main business of the college teaching.
(*e*) There is a very wide range of written information on careers available ranging from comprehensive but inevitably slightly out of date encyclopaedias on courses and careers to simple handouts duplicated in schools.

V. Semicolons (;)

The semicolon has two distinct uses.

Use 1. It can be employed to separate items in a series (as an alternative to Use 1 of the comma) where commas are not felt to be strong enough. This may be because the series is very long or because the items are rather complicated and/or include commas themselves.

Example 1: *The three main ways of distributing consumer goods in their near-finished state to the consumer can be described as follows: the manufacturer, grower, or importer can sell to a retail organisation; he can sell to a wholesaler who in turn then resells to a retailer; he can sell directly to the consumer.*

Use 2. The semicolon can also be used as a sentence-joining device. Two sentences that could be joined by linking as discussed in Chapter 14 may also be joined by a semicolon. (Three sentences can be joined by two semicolons, four by three semicolons etc.)

Example 1: *He was in a hurry to finish the job; he nailed the crate down with insufficient care.*

Example 2: *The assistant refused to change the gloves; they had been damaged.*

The sentences thus joined must be very close to each other in sense, and the second should follow logically upon the first The effect of using semicolons instead of normal linking is to speed up what we write, but at the cost of making it seem a little jerky. Semicolons provide a useful variant – and those who tend to fuse their sentences together would avoid many sentence errors if they could remember to put a semicolon instead of a comma between the two sentences thus thrust together.

Exercise 38
A. The following fused sentences can be corrected by replacing one comma by either a full stop or a semicolon. Where should this come? Which do you prefer, the full stop or the semicolon? Justify the use of each remaining comma.

(a) The importance of communication cannot be over-emphasised, whether it is applied to customer relations or in the individual's personal relationships, the task is basically the same and anything that reduces the frustration, unhappiness, and friction that are the results of misunderstanding is worthwhile.

(b) Radios and small electric fires have a very similar rate of retail stock turnover, both require skilled retailing and both are usually branded, but the retail margin on radios, although they are usually of a higher unit value, is greater than that on small fires.

B. Punctuate the following sentences in what seems to you the most effective way.

(a) The big department stores have special training sections complete with rooms for lectures discussions demonstrations and displays for the first few months young sales assistants spend part of their time in such a section.

(b) A college librarian interested in career advice should ensure that his library contains books of general interest on careers including biographies a series of books on careers written by practitioners and background books on the major industries of the country which several publishers are now producing many designed for students of limited academic ability who want to know what happens behind the scenes in for example a shop or a warehouse.

(c) It is estimated that there are some 60 000 occupations in this country depending upon how delicately one distinguishes between different branches of for example engineering there are over 200 careers which require some definite academic standard on entry and provide for training leading to a recognised qualification.

VI. Colons (:)

Colons are used before (*a*) an example, (*b*) a series of items, or (*c*) a quotation, for which the Rx has been prepared by some introductory words.

(*a*) This book includes many examples introduced in this way. There is one in the next but one sentence.

(*b*) Example 1 on page 136 includes a colon preceding a series of items.

(*c*) The following example demonstrates the use of the colon to introduce a quotation:

> *The actual words used in the regulations are: 'Entry must always be made, and fees paid, to the centre which has agreed to accommodate a candidate'.*

Until fairly recently the colon was also often employed as a sort of super semicolon but this use is dying out rapidly. You will meet examples of this in what you read but should not attempt to use it this way yourself.

VII. Inverted commas (quotation marks)

A. Inverted commas may be single ('...') or double ("...."). There is no rule about which to use but single ones are more popular today.

B. They are used as we saw in the example at the end of the previous section – to mark out words quoted either from writing or from speech. Quotations from written material are usually introduced by a colon but a comma is generally used with spoken words. As the words between the inverted commas must all be quoted words we have to be careful to arrange that no other words (such as those telling the Rx who is speaking) come between them. Look at the following examples very carefully, noting particularly the use of commas in association with inverted commas.

Example 1: *The assistant said, 'I am unable to change these gloves as they have been damaged.'*

Example 2: *'I am unable to change these gloves as they have been damaged,' said the assistant.*

Example 3: *'I am unable to change these gloves,' said the assistant, 'as they have been damaged.'*

Example 4: *'I am unable to change these gloves,' said the assistant. 'They have been damaged.'*

For discussion
Why is Example 3 different from Example 4 in its punctuation?

C. Inverted commas (as we have already noted earlier in the course) are used round technical words, or slang when there is no proper written equivalent available. Such inverted commas mean 'so-called' or 'as we say'. Never use inverted commas to give emphasis.

For discussion
What is wrong with the following showcard?

SPECIAL OFFER OF 'LEATHER' NOTECASES

D. Inverted commas are also used to indicate the titles of books, plays, films etc.: the names of newspapers and magazines; the names of ships, locomotives etc. For placing the inverted commas correctly it is necessary to know if a *the* in such a title or name is part of it or not – thus *'The Times'* but the *'Radio Times'*.

Exercise 39
Write out the names of all the daily newspapers you can think of, using inverted commas. Include the word *the* with each.

VIII. Apostrophes

A. Apostrophes are used to indicate missing letters in words. Thus *three o'clock* (three of the clock) *can't* (cannot) *I'll* (I shall) etc.
NOTE. It's (it is or it has) but *its* (of it). Similarly, *hers, ours, yours, theirs* have no apostrophe.

B. We show possession by using *'s* (*Mr Brown's office* – the office of, or belonging to, Mr Brown) unless the basic word is a plural ending in *s* when we add the apostrophe only (*Ladies' Room*). People get into a terrible tangle with *'s* but, as you see, the rule is quite simple. Sometimes people become so nervous about *'s* that they put an apostrophe somewhere at the end of every plural ending in *s* – even when there is no question of 'of, or belonging to'.

For discussion
What is wrong with the following showcard?

SPECIAL OFFER OF LEATHER NOTECASES'

One special uncertainty about the use of *'s* that may well concern users of this book is whether or not to use an apostrophe in the names of shops and firms (i.e. should we write *Boot's* or *Boots*?). Logic indicates that the apostrophe should be used (since what is meant is 'Boot's shop') but in practice the form without the apostrophe is more common – perhaps because the apostrophe looks awkward in display material.

You may like to carry out your own investigation, noting from the fascia boards of shops, firms' letterheads, advertising material etc., how many shops and firms with trading names of this kind use an apostrophe and how many do not.

In this book the apostrophe is not used in names of shops and firms.

Exercise 40
Put in apostrophes as necessary in the following expressions and sentences. Be careful not to put in any that are not required.

(*a*) The party is at Harrys place.
(*b*) I cant change these gloves.

(*c*) Yours faithfully,
(*d*) The Students Union
(*e*) FRESHLY MADE PORK PIES
(*f*) Its a long time since I last saw you.
(*g*) With a new car you should keep a record of all petrol bought so that you can check its mileage to the gallon.
(*h*) The customers handbag.
(*i*) The customers six handbags.
(*j*) The six customers handbags.
(*k*) Among the many doubtful tales told of Shakespeares early life there is the one that asserts that he made a living by holding horses heads for gentlemen visiting the theatre.

IX. Exclamation marks (!) Question marks (?)

A. Sometimes an exclamation mark is essential.

How they all laughed! is a sentence.
How they all laughed. is not a sentence.

They are also necessary after exclamations (*Well! Oh!*) and words indicating noises (*Wham! Whoosh!*) or shouts (*Quiet! Help!*).

They have little use in business outside advertising material but are sometimes used to add emphasis to a notice or showcard:

SPECIAL PURCHASE – ONLY 50P EACH!

Many people think such statements are just as effective without the exclamation mark and look more dignified. One trouble with employing exclamation marks to give emphasis is that if you use them a great deal they lose their effect on the Rx. Never try to increase the emphasis by using double or triple exclamation marks – they look comic.

B. Question marks are used after direct questions only (i.e. the actual questioning words, not a version of them):

Mr Brown asked, 'Where did you put the invoice?' (direct question)

BUT

Mr Brown asked me where I had put the invoice (indirect question).

Remember if you ask a direct question in something you write it must have its question mark. For example, in a letter:

Which are your delivery days for Shrivenham? (direct question)

BUT

I should like to know which are your delivery days for Shrivenham (indirect question).

18
Writing Letters

I. Basic points

In your letters you have your best opportunity to put into practice what you have learned about writing to communicate. The two most important questions to ask yourself about any letter you write are:

1. Will the Rx understand it?
2. Will it produce the response I want?

To turn to less vital matters (but still very important) you should try to avoid wasting words or putting in irrelevant material. Personal letters are rather different here, but business letters at least should be as brief as is possible without reducing communication. Yet even in business correspondence it is always worth while putting in a few extra words that make your letter seem more polite, more friendly, or more human. You will try to pick language that is appropriate in tone to the kind of letter you are writing. You will also want to write correctly – at least in business letters. These often pass through many hands and it is not pleasant to think that several people may be laughing at you because of mistakes in your letter.

Finally, so that your letter looks a 'proper' letter, you will want to use the layout and conventions appropriate to the kind of letter you are writing. By 'layout' we mean how the letter, whether handwritten or typed, is arranged on the paper; by 'conventions' we mean the devices that have been generally agreed upon over the years for showing the date, to whom the letter is directed, addresses etc.

II. Personal letters

Personal letters (to friends and relations) present few problems.

Layout and conventions (which you have to be very careful with for business letters) are simple – and not always observed. All you have to do is to put your address in the top righthand corner of the letter with the date beneath. The address on handwritten letters is usually written in such

Example

9. Valley Road,
Timberley,
SWINDON, Wiltshire,
SN4 2QG
18 February, 19. .

Dear Jack,

Thanks for your letter— it was good to hear from you. You seem to be having a pretty fair time of it since you moved. I'm quite envious. I'd no idea there were so many pretty girls in those parts. Sounds a regular bird fancier's paradise.

If you can tear yourself away from all those delights, Tom and I were wondering if you would join us for a short youth-hostelling trip at Easter. We shall be walking. I hope that doesn't frighten you off! Plans are a bit vague at the moment but we thought that the Sussex downs would be easy walking and about right for both sides to get to. Perhaps we could rendezvous at Arundel on Good Friday. Could you hitch your way there by opening time? (Hostel opening time, I mean!).

Let me know if you like the idea, and Tom and I will work out a more detailed programme. We'll have to get moving or all the hostels will be booked up.

All the best,

Paul

a way that each line of it starts a little to the right of the line above in the style known as 'progressive indent'. The example on page 142 shows this.

The 'subscription', the word or two you use (on a separate line) to finish the letter off before you put your name (on the line below), can be almost anything that seems to you appropriate. The more usual ways of signing off include: *Yours sincerely; Love; Yours affectionately; With best wishes; All the best.* As they are personal letters it does not really matter what you put – but some people do not much care for receiving letters that end *Cheerio; Bye-bye for now: Mud in your eye* etc., even from friends or relatives. If it is the kind of personal letter that is almost a business letter (as when writing to your former headmaster for a reference) or to somebody you do not know well, it is best to use *Yours sincerely.* Such letters are called 'semi-formal'. Do note the capital letter that starts all these subscriptions, even the most informal.

The language of the completely personal letter is very easygoing. You really want to sound as if you are speaking to your friend so colloquialisms and slang are in order. In the semi-formal letter, however, you should avoid colloquialisms.

Personal letters may be written for many reasons. Often it is just a matter of keeping in touch with somebody whom you no longer see, probably because they live a long distance away from you. The communication element in such letters is small. Your motive in writing is to let the other person know you have not forgotten them and to tell them a little about what you are doing so that *they* do not forget *you.* You should try to make such letters interesting to read – otherwise the other person may stop writing because your letters are not worth receiving. Even in such a simple type of letter as this, however, you should remember your basic communication principles and ask yourself: *Why am I writing? What kind of person am I writing to? What will he/she be interested in?*

Other personal letters may have a much higher communication content. You may be writing to thank somebody for a present; to tell them how sorry you are they are ill; to arrange a meeting; to pass on some special piece of news. The example on page 142 is of this type.

In all handwritten letters, the handwriting should be legible. Particular care should be taken to make sure your address is clearly written. The name of the post town, and the postcode, should be in capitals.

For discussion

1. Do you consider that Paul has dealt with all the points that Jack would need to know at this stage of the arrangements?
2. Is his language appropriate to this sort of letter?

Exercise 41

Imagine you have a close friend (same sex as yourself) who moved from your area several months ago and to whom you send occasional letters describing what you have been doing. Write one such letter. It should be about 150 words long (not counting the address).

Exercise 42

A friend of yours who has left the area is shortly to return. He/she is considering seeking employment similar to yours at your place of work. Write to give him/her some idea of your daily routine and what working conditions are like. Do not exceed 200 words.

III. Business letters – conventions and layout

Business letters are always much more formal than personal ones, and detailed attention must be given to the traditional conventions and layout. Such details – trivial though they are in themselves – play quite an important communication role. They are the recognised hallmarks of the business letter. A letter that does not observe them seems to many people not to be a 'proper' business letter, and it may be treated with less than full seriousness as a result. A letter which does not keep to the rules may therefore fail to communicate as effectively as one that does.

The principal conventions and layout points are outlined below, followed by two specimen layouts (pages 148 and 149). Do not forget that these points apply not only to any letters you may be required to write in the future in connection with your work, but also to every letter that you write to a firm as a private person.

THE INSIDE ADDRESS

This constitutes the most obvious difference between a business letter and a personal letter. At the upper lefthand side of the first sheet of a business letter immediately below the line on which the date is shown (on the opposite side) is written the name and address of the firm or individual to whom the letter is being sent (see specimen layouts). Originally a device to ensure that the carbon copy retained by the sender automatically indicated to whom the letter had been addressed, it has become a convention that is used even when no carbon copy is being made.

The specimen layouts show typical inside addressing to firms. If the letter is going to a private person the method is a little different. If he is male his name will almost certainly be shown, at the inside address and on the envelope, followed by *Esq.* (the abbreviation of *Esquire*), thus:

J. Middleton Esq.,
5 Plenty Street,
BATH,
Somerset.
BA8 5JK

Of course, this is quite absurd – but while the majority of people believe it is more polite to be addressed this way in a formal letter than as *Mr* . . . . . . the convention is not going to change. A curiosity about the use of *Esq.* is that it can only be used if the initials or first name/s of the addressee are shown. If you do not know these (and with customers you often do not) you have to use *Mr* anyway. There is no equivalent for ladies, who can be addressed only as *Mrs* or *Miss*.

THE SALUTATION

1. If the letter is addressed to the whole firm the salutation is plural –
   Dear Sirs.
2. Sometimes one wishes to route a letter to a firm into a particular
   section or department. You may do this by addressing it to the head of
   that section or department. It should always be addressed to the top
   man, and he is normally addressed by his title not his name, thus:

The Catering Manager,
   New Market Hotels Ltd,
      Lea Road, LONDON.
         SE14 9JM

Dear Sir,

NOTE (*a*) the capital letters used in the addressee's title (*b*) the salutation
Dear Sir, (singular because only one person is being addressed this
time).

3. For formal business letters to individuals the salutation is usually *Dear
   Sir,* or *Dear Madam,*. If the letter is not fully formal (usually this means
   that you know the person you are writing to at least slightly – from,
   for example, visits to your store, hotel, salon etc.) the salutation should
   be *Dear Mr–Dear Mrs*–or *Dear Miss*–a more friendly type of salutation. (There are a number of specialised variants, of which the most
   common are *Dear Reverend*–for clergymen and *Dear Doctor*–for all
   those holding doctorates – not only those of medicine).

THE DATE

The two most widely accepted ways of dating formal letters are *20th
November, 19..* and the slightly more modern *20 November, 19..* . The
comma after the month is increasingly omitted these days – but if you
decide to do this you should be consistent. You are strongly advised to
make a habit of using one of these methods in all your business letters,
although they are not the only possible ones. *Not acceptable* are: (1) using
only numerals (2) putting only the last two numerals of the year (i.e.
leaving out the *19*).

Many people consider it looks better if the name of the month is always
put in full. Certainly you should never attempt to abbreviate *May, June,*
and *July.*

POSTCODES

At the time of writing postcodes are not essential parts of addresses as
automatic sorting has not started, but the Post Office is encouraging
everybody to use them. Business houses are setting a good example, but
the codes are not so universally used as the examples in this book imply. It
seems best, however, to anticipate future developments by getting into the
habit of using postcodes immediately.

An explanation of the purpose and use of postcodes is provided in
Appendix 3 of this book (page 175).

THE SUBSCRIPTION

The subscription *Yours faithfully,* is correct in completely formal business letters (i.e. those with the salutation *Dear Sir,* etc.). *Yours sincerely,* is correct for less formal business letters (i.e. those with the salutation *Dear Mr—*). Do not attempt to use any subscription other than one of these two in your business letters. (There are other subscriptions which are correct under certain circumstances – but you make life unnecessarily complicated for yourself by bothering with them.)

LAYOUT

1. A business letter should not look cramped. One-line spaces at the following points improve appearance and clarity: (*a*) between Tx's address and date (*b*) between date line and first line of inside address (*c*) between inside address and salutation. In typewritten letters these spacings are usually more generous than this. (See specimen layouts.)

2. Students are sometimes worried by the waste of space at the top lefthand corner of the paper but this is part of the accepted style. References are put over this side (opposite the date, on the same line) taking up part of this space. It is also used for special instructions such as: *For the attention of Mr Holmes.* (This, by the way, is the method by which the Tx ensures that the comparatively low-ranked person who dealt with him personally receives the letter that by the rules has to be addressed to his boss. It is also the way assistants get credit – and commission – for orders sent in by post as a follow-up to good selling on the sales floor.)

3. Paragraphs should all be indented the same distance. For handwritten letters some people place the first letter of the first word of the first paragraph exactly under the comma of the salutation, and line the other paragraphs up accordingly. This can produce a very neat effect; but if your handwriting is rather large, or the salutation is a long one, the indentations may then be wastefully deep. Common sense must be your guide. All paragraphs of a typewritten letter are indented a fixed distance (usually five spaces).

   A surprising number of students forget to indent the first paragraph altogether.

4. In the past the convention has been that in handwritten letters addresses (both inside and on the envelope) are shown in 'progressive indent' style, but in typewritten letters 'block' style is used (i.e. each line starts the same distance from the lefthand margin as the previous line – see example on page 144 and specimen layout on page 149). The convention is observed in the examples in this book but it should be pointed out that 'block' style is becoming increasingly popular for all business letters, even handwritten ones.

5. The subscription is normally centred for typewritten letters, but placed rather to the right of centre for handwritten letters.

Simplified layouts for typed business letters have been experimented with by some firms over the last few years – but this is a field in which anything new takes a long time to be accepted.

Typewritten layouts are referred to only because you will receive such letters and find the differences confusing if not mentioned. Most readers of this book will only have to produce handwritten letters and those few who do type letters will have had typing classes in which letter layouts have been fully treated.

SPECIMEN LAYOUTS

A. Private person to firm

B. Firm to firm

Notes on specimen layouts

1. Addresses are shown with conventional punctuation – a comma after each line and a full stop after the county. 'Open' style, omitting the punctuation at the end of each line of the address is slowly gaining support as an alternative form that is a little less trouble and looks a little neater. You may take your pick – but you must not mix these two styles in the same letter.

2. Postcodes are shown, in capitals, on a separate line. An alternative position – for use only if the address is unusually long – is on the same line as the county but separated from it by a distinct space.

3. The address on the envelope should use the same wording and layout style as that on the letter, but, as there is more room, should be spaced out.

4. Something over which there is much confusion, especially in retailing, is the use of *Messrs*. This is an abbreviation of *Messieurs* still in use as a sort of plural of *Mr,* and up to a few years ago regularly used in front of the trading names of firms where these consisted of the names of the partners. Most firms are now limited companies and *Messrs* is not considered appropriate before the name of a limited company. Thus when there were two men, a Mr Lightfoot and a Mr Friskit, trading in partnership to run a shoe shop they could have been correctly addressed, together, as *Messrs Lightfoot and Friskit* (just as each could have been called – separately – *Mr*). But once they became *Lightfoot, Friskit and Co. Ltd* (or *Lightfoot and Friskit Ltd*) *Messrs* could no longer be used. Few simple partnerships remain, and therefore few opportunities to use *Messrs* correctly – but old habits die hard and it tends to be slipped in rather frequently when it is not needed, especially by shops and stores when referring to each other.

5. Firms use stationery with a printed head to ensure that – at the minimum – all letters from the firm show its correct trading name and address. Much more information (telephone numbers, telegraphic address, names of directors, even an advertising slogan or picture of the works) may be included. The address is frequently centred under the firm's name – as in the specimen layout – but it may also appear in the normal top righthand position. There are many variants and you should collect a number of examples of firms' stationery to compare.

A. Private person to firm

7 Greening Cottages,
Diddlings,
WAREHAM,
Dorset.
BH 20 7JK

15th January, 19..

Lightfoot, Friskit and Co. Ltd.,
15-17 Tripping Lane,
BOURNEMOUTH,
Dorset.
BH2   3JS

Dear Sirs,

_____

_____ .

_____

_____

_____ .

_____

_____

_____ .

Yours faithfully,
Joseph Soap

B. Firm to firm

THE TOEFIT SHOE COMPANY LTD.
LEATHER AVENUE　　　**NORTHAMPTON**　　　**NN3 2MB**

Our ref: NJ/221X　　　　　15 January, 19..
Your ref: JKL/MNF

Lightfoot, Friskit and Co. Ltd

15-17 Tripping Lane,

BOURNEMOUTH,

Dorset.

BH2 3JS

Dear Sirs,

　　　　　　TUF-TOP walking shoes

　　　　Yours faithfully,

　　　A Stitch

　　　　A. Stitch

　　　　　Sales Manager

6. A firm will always give a reference to correspondence, and this is intended for quotation in the reply. This ensures that the reply goes to the right man, or in a large organisation may be the key to a complicated filing system. The simplest reference consists of the initials of the man sending the letter combined with those of the girl typing it. Lightfoot and Friskit's reference (on their previous letter) must have been of this kind. The Toefit Shoe Company's own reference illustrates one of many types of filing key reference number. When firm writes to firm each will have to give a reference to the correspondence and to avoid confusion these are marked *Our ref.* and *Your ref.* (The full stop to indicate that *ref.* is an abbreviation for *reference* is in fact nowadays usually omitted, as in our example.)

7. A 'subject head' is shown in the example, but these are not, of course, always used in letters from firms. The advantage of a subject head is that it gives a convenient label to the letter, quickly indicating its subject matter and whose responsibility it is (if, for example, the person whose reference is on the letter is not available when the reply comes). Where a correspondence is exchanged between two parties and one party gives a subject head to the correspondence, this should be repeated by the other party so that the letters from both sides bear the same 'label'. The subject head should appear on the line below the *Dear Sir,* and be centred and underlined. The *Re* that some old-fashioned shops, stores, salons etc. put in front of the subject head serves no purpose and should not be used – unless your boss insists on it!

8. A firm's letter may be signed in a number of ways, according to the degree of importance given to the correspondence. In ascending order the most common are:

(*a*) name of firm only;
(*b*) name of firm plus initials of Tx;
(*c*) name of firm plus signature;
(*d*) signature with office held (as example).

IV. Business letters – style

Whenever you write a letter on behalf of your firm you should remember that your firm will be judged by the way you write. When you write to a firm on your own behalf you should remember that how that firm treats you will largely depend upon the way you write.

As the Tx you must remember your communication principles and, whenever you have a chance, try to suit your vocabulary and sentence length to the Rx. You judge this by such clues as your previous dealings with him; what sort of person he seemed when you met him in shop, store, salon, restaurant, or hotel; what he sounded like on the telephone; what sort of letter he has written to you etc.

You will wish your letter to seem dignified and correct – but not stuffy. You will therefore write in well-constructed sentences and pick your words with care.

Starting the letter off is sometimes difficult. A subject head helps here, but you should avoid referring to this in your first sentence by such clumsy expressions as *I am writing to you about the above.*

When you reply to a letter, you should first acknowledge this and quote its date. Simple opening sentences such as *Thank you for your letter of 15th January*, or *We were sorry to receive your complaint of 15th January* are best. If you quote the date of the letter, its reference, and its subject head (if there was one), there is not much point in starting your reply with a summary of the letter to which you are replying, but an amazing number of people do.

Openings involving such phrases as *With reference to* and *Referring to* are best avoided. Thus *With reference to your enquiry of 15th January concerning TUF-TOP walking shoes, we have pleasure in enclosing an illustrated leaflet which we hope will provide all the information you require* is much inferior to its modern equivalent: *Thank you for your enquiry of 15th January. We are enclosing an illustrated leaflet which we hope will provide all the information that you require about TUF-TOP walking shoes.* People who are addicted to this form of opening also all too often produce non-sentences of the type: *Referring to your enquiry of 15th January concerning TUF-TOP walking shoes.*

At the end of the letter it is a good idea to try to put in some helpful sort of remark such as: *If you still feel at all uncertain about this matter, please do not hesitate to write to us again* before the subscription. If you cannot think of something useful to say it is better to say nothing, even if the letter seems to end rather abruptly. A final sentence such as *We assure you of our sincere desire to be of fullest assistance to you at all times* is just a meaningless collection of words, ignored by the Rx, and better omitted altogether.

Some old fashioned business people insert before the subscription a separate line *I am,* or *We are.* There is no point in this unless the letter ends with a construction based on a present participle and these words are necessary to complete the sentence, as in:

> *Awaiting your further instructions,*
> *We are,*
> *Yours faithfully,*

However, these participal endings are invariably oldfashioned and better replaced by a straightforward modern sentence.

> *We await your further instructions.*
> *Yours faithfully,*

sounds much brisker. So there does not seem to be any future for *I am,* and *We are,* endings.

There is no such thing as a special 'business English' used in business letters. Something of the kind did exist in the Edwardian period at the beginning of this century, and was particularly popular with shops, stores, and hotels. It was an unpleasantly obsequious language full of *humbles* and *respectfuls* and *begs,* with a few scraps of Latin to make it sound grand. Fragments of oldfashioned shopkeeper's language still turn up from time to time and you should guard against picking up the habit of using them. Unfortunately it is often the keenest young learners who start using these undesirable expressions, mistakenly thinking that they add a professional touch to their letters. The table below is intended (1) to warn you which expressions you should avoid (2) to provide a translation in case you come across them in letters and do not know what they mean.

EDWARDIAN EXPRESSION	MODERN EQUIVALENT
inst., ult., prox.	Name of present, previous or following month, respectively
re	*about*
per	*by*
as per	*as in* or *as stated in*
your favour	*your order* (*letter*)
prior to	*before*
same	*this, it*
please advise us (*me*)	*please let us* (*me*) *know*
Enclosed please find	*We* (*I*) *enclose*
We beg to . . . *We have the honour to . . .* *We respectfully . . .*	Crawling – omit
Yours respectfully, *and oblige* (used as a subscription)	Crawling – use *Yours faithfully, Yours faithfully, Yours sincerely,*
We have to acknowledge the receipt of . . . *We are in receipt of . . .*	*We have received . . .* or *Thank you for . . .*
Assuring you of our best attention at all times, *Trusting this action meets with your approval,* etc	Omit, or substitute a more sincere sounding complete sentence (i.e. not starting with a present participle)
Thanking you in anticipation (or *in advance*),	As above, but specially unsatisfactory because you are assuming that the Rx is going to do what you want before he has had a chance to reply.

The specimen correspondence that follows illustrates the modern style in business letters – dignified, but not stiff or unnatural. For people who do not very often have to do it writing a business letter is something of an ordeal. This should not be made apparent to the Rx – a good business letter should seem relaxed and confident.

Handwriting is represented by italic type in these, and subsequent, examples of letters.

V. A specimen correspondence

1.

55 Cod Street,
FRASERBURGH,
Aberdeenshire,
AB4 8YZ
12th May, 19 . .

Rassemblit Ltd,
Bridal Street,
HITCHIN, Herts.
SG4 8DF

Dear Sirs,
I purchased from you about two years ago one of your Unifix quick-assembly armchairs. It has been perfectly satisfactory until yesterday when one of the fixing rings broke away from the square rubber springing that forms the base of the seat. The rubber is torn at the point where the ring came away and this apparently minor fault has made the chair useless.
In view of the time I have had the chair I do not know whether you will consider this a defect of a kind that merits free replacement, but I am anxious to have the chair back in use again quickly even if this has to be at my own expense. Please let me have your comments and suggestions as soon as possible.
The invoice reference number was BA/1512/Z2.

Yours faithfully,

J. Fisher

2.

RASSEMBLIT LTD

Bridal Street, HITCHIN, Herts. SG4 8DF

AKP/V/541

15th May, 19..

J. Fisher, Esq.,
55 Cod Street,
FRASERBURGH,
Aberdeenshire,
AB4 8YZ

Dear Sir,

I am very sorry to learn from your letter of 12th May that the trampoline base to your Unifix chair has proved defective. We certainly expect

these bases to last very much longer than two
years and I am instructing our despatch department
to send you a replacement trampoline immediately.

I should be extremely obliged if you would be so
good as to post the faulty trampoline to us, addressed
for my attention, so that we can check the nature
of the defect and take the matter up with our sub-
contractors. We shall, of course, refund your
postage if you will let us know how much this is.

Yours faithfully,

A. K. Penrose
Adjustments Manager

3.

55 *Cod Street,*
FRASERBURGH,
Aberdeenshire.
AB4 8YZ
21st May, 19 . .

AKP/V/541

The Adjustments Manager,
Rassemblit Ltd,
Bridal Street,
HITCHIN, Herts.
SG4 8DF

Dear Sir,
Thank you for your letter of 15th May. I consider that I have been very
fairly treated by your firm in this matter.
I have now received the replacement trampoline and fitted this
successfully. I have today posted the faulty trampoline to you. The
postage was 48p.

Yours faithfully,

J. Fisher

4.

55 Cod Street,
FRASERBURGH,
Aberdeenshire.
AB4 8YZ
20th June 19 . .

AKP/V/541

The Adjustments Manager,
*   Rassemblit Ltd,*
*   Bridal Street,*
*   HITCHIN, Herts.*
*   SG4 8DF*

Dear Sir,
    I feel some hesitation in writing to you again as your firm has treated me generously over the matter of the faulty trampoline on my Unifix chair. However it was agreed that my postage would be refunded if I returned the trampoline. I did this but have not received the refund of postage. I feel sure there must be some oversight here and that I ought to draw your attention to it.

Yours faithfully,

J. Fisher

5.

RASSEMBLIT LTD

Bridal Street, HITCHIN, Herts. SG4 8DF

AKP/V/541   22nd June, 19..

J. Fisher, Esq.,
33 Cod Street,
FRASERBURGH,
Aberdeenshire,
AB4 8YZ

Dear Sir,

    Thank you for your letter of 20th May. I must apologise that there has been this delay in refunding your postage. I have checked with our Accounts Department and a postal order for 48p will be despatched to you within twenty-four hours.

Yours faithfully,

A. K. Penrose

Adjustments Manager

NOTES:

Letter 1

(*a*) Quick assembly furniture is sold in separate units that have to be assembled by the customer. Fisher's particular type of chair has its seat cushion resting on a thick rubber square which, when the chair is assembled, is stretched across the chair frame at the top of the legs and attached to hooks by four metal rings at the corners of the square. Fisher has a communication problem – he does not know the technical term for this rubber square.

(*b*) Fisher's letter is very reasonable in attitude. He also includes all necessary information to permit action, including the invoice reference number that will enable the firm to check the date of purchase.

Letter 2

(*a*) The replies to letters of complaint are called 'letters of adjustment' or 'adjustment letters'. Rassemblit have an Adjustments Manager to deal with such letters. With small firms there is no specialist department to deal with complaints and the task may fall to almost anybody.

There is more to adjustments than writing letters. On receipt of a letter of complaint the first task is to find out if the complaint is justified. If it is, the next is to decide what action to take to put the matter right as far as possible. Finally a tactful letter has to be written apologising, and explaining what action is being taken (as here). If the complaint is not justified (the customer has, for example, not read the instructions; or has used the article for months and now expects a new one; or has broken it through misuse) the firm's position is more difficult. The letter then sent is very difficult to write as the firm must refuse to act, while not making the customer appear either a fool or a rogue.

(*b*) Notice how smoothly Penrose slips the technical term *trampoline* into the correspondence without making Fisher feel ignorant for not knowing it.

(*c*) The tone of the letter is reassuring and indicates a genuine desire to put the matter right. At the same time by asking for the return of the trampoline Penrose to some extent protects his firm against misrepresentation by the customer. After all, the trampoline may have failed because Fisher's son slashed it with a flick knife! He could protect his firm much better by offering to send the replacement trampoline only on receipt of the defective one. This would, however, increase the time that Fisher was deprived of the use of his chair. Penrose would decide which action to take on the basis of the sort of letter of complaint received. Fisher's seems at once businesslike and honest and is therefore treated on its face value.

Letter 5

Penrose does not waste time trying to explain where there has been a slip-up. He apologises and sees to it that the matter is put right without delay.

Exercise 43

Write (*a*) a letter to a firm of your choice (real or imaginary) complaining about either a product purchased or service, and (*b*) the firm's reply. Add all details necessary to make the two letters convincing. It is to be assumed that your complaint is justified.

Exercise 44

Write a similar letter of complaint to the one in Exercise 43 and the firm's reply, assuming that the firm decides that your complaint is not justified. You may prefer to pretend to be somebody else for this exercise.

Exercise 45

You are employed as hotel receptionist at the Blue Boar, Memsbury. The owner passes the following letter to you. This is what he says to you about it:

This is a bit awkward. We put the price up a fortnight ago and I suppose we should have rung the paper and tried to get them to change that bit of the advert. The trouble is we've paid for ten weekly insertions and I think there are still three to go. He's got rather a point about the coffee too. I think we'd better cancel the rest of those adverts and try to get the 'Advertiser' to give us a credit. Then we'll reword the advert to make the price right and bring in this chap's idea about the coffee and run another ten insertions. Write this chap Price a nice letter. Write to the 'Pidderminster Advertiser' for me too. I'll sign both of them myself, so write as if the letters are coming from me. Tell the 'Advertiser' how we want the wording altered – that will save having to write a second time. We'll keep the coffee as an extra I think – some people don't want coffee and they'd resent having to pay for it if they weren't having it.

> 16 College Street,
> PIDDERMINSTER,
> Somerset.
> BA25 4BJ
> 15th June, 19 . .

The Proprietor,
   The Blue Boar,
      MEMSBURY,
         Somerset.
            BA17 3KN

Dear Sir,
    You have been advertising dinner at the Blue Boar for several weeks as '£1.50 – all courses included' and in fact these words appear in your advertisement in today's 'Pidderminster Advertiser'. When I dined at your hotel on 8th June I was charged £1.80. The menu had been altered to this price in ink.

A further point that I find unsatisfactory is that coffee was charged as a 15p extra. I think that 'all courses included' implies that coffee is included in the price. It was only a three course dinner and 'all' is not a word one would normally use for three. To remove all possibility of ambiguity from your advertisement I consider that you should either include the coffee in the price and make it clear that it is included, or keep the coffee as an extra but state that it is an extra in the wording of the advertisement.

I would welcome your comments on these two points.

Yours faithfully,

John Price

VI. Letters of application

When you apply for a post there are certain details about yourself that the prospective employer is bound to want to know – your age, whether married or single, education, qualifications obtained, present post and/or present course, previous experience, if any, and special interests, if relevant. He will also want the names, status, and addresses of one or two people whom he can ask about you. These people are called 'referees' – because he can refer to them. It is up to you whether you incorporate all these points in the main body of your letter along with some reference to the particular job you are applying for and where you saw it advertised, or whether you write a very brief formal letter of application and enclose a well-organised summary of the points mentioned. If you choose the second method you will simply write something like *I wish to apply for the post of ---- advertised in ---- of (date) and enclose a summary of my personal details.* The enclosed details should have a general heading such as *Personal Details – John Smith,* and the material should be laid out neatly under subheadings such as *Education, Previous Experience* etc. Start with your full name and address and, if possible, a telephone number where you can be reached.

Exercise 46
Prepare an advertisement for the kind of job you hope to get at the end of the course you are now on. Then, using one of the two methods referred to above, write the letter of application.

Exercise 47
Write a letter to your old headmaster or present head of department (but assuming you have left the college) asking him to agree to act as a referee for you. You should tell him something about the post you are applying for, or, if you have no particular post in mind, what type of job you will be putting in for.

VII. Letters to the Editor

Letters to newspapers and magazines do not differ essentially from other formal letters. They are addressed to *The Editor* and may be signed *Yours faithfully,* or *Yours etc.,.* The latter is a curious form based on the practice of newspapers in the past of putting *Yours etc.,* as the subscription to all letters printed in order to avoid having to show all the various sub-scriptions people had actually used. Nowadays it is rare to see any subscription printed – space is saved by simply printing the writer's name.

Exercise 48
Write a letter of about 150 words to the editor of the newspaper of the town you are to imagine you live in giving your views on one of the following matters of local controversy:
(a) The routing of a much-needed relief road through the beautiful old park that is the only open space other than playing fields in the built-up part of the own.
(b) The loneliness and neglect suffered by old people and what can be done about it.
(c) An article in the newspaper the previous day suggesting that young people have no interest in their town.

VIII. Further letter practice

NOTE. In this group of exercises you are required to invent such details, including names and addresses, as would be known in a real-life situation.

Exercise 49
You work in a supermarket. Write a letter to a friend who works in a small individually owned shop explaining to him the sort of differences between your work and his.
    If you prefer, you can attempt this exercise the other way round (i.e. it is the Rx who works in the supermarket).

Exercise 50
You work in a hairdressing salon. A very distressed letter has been received from a valued customer of long standing asserting that following the use of a DYEPICK auburn dye at the salon the previous day her hair has turned green. The owner of the salon knows you have been attending Communi-cation classes and asks you to draft out, for her signature, a letter to the customer and one to Dyepick. What she says is: *Write and calm her down and say how sorry we are. Ask her to come in so that we can examine her hair. I expect she feels embarrassed. Don't put anything in at this stage that looks as if we are accepting responsibility, though. Then write to Dyepick. Find out if it's ever happened before; if it's possible that it could happen. Ask them what they advise us to do.*

Exercise 51
Write the following series of three letters:

(a) To a hotel (or boarding-house) enquiring what accommodation they can offer you for your summer holiday (give dates) and requesting details of tariff.

(*b*) The hotel's reply.

(*c*) Your reply confirming booking.

NOTE. The person to write to at a hotel is *The Proprietor* if the hotel is privately owned, *The Manager* if it is one of a chain.

Exercise 52

You are the secretary of a large club and you wish to make arrangements for the club dinner. You expect about 150 people to attend.

Write the following series of three letters:

(*a*) To a restaurant or hotel asking whether they can accommodate so large a group and asking for suggested menus and prices. Give alternative dates and ask what kind of room is available.

(*b*) The reply to this letter (assuming they can accommodate your club).

(*c*) Your reply, accepting one of the suggestions made and confirming the date.

19
Further Applications and Communication Practice

I. Postcards

Postcards are one type of written communication with customers that quite junior staff may sometimes be required to write. Many firms keep, of course, a stock of preprinted cards to suit standard situations; these leave only such details as times, dates, the name of the item referred to etc. to be written in by hand.

Business postcards are much more informal than business letters. There is no equivalent to the inside addressing (after all, the name and address of the Rx is only on the other side of the card), and a subscription is also unnecessary. They are not usually signed, initialling normally being considered sufficient. The date may appear top right, as on letters, but may be placed bottom left. It is often shown in an abbreviated form that would be frowned on in a business letter. Preprinted cards are often marked *Date as postmark* to save time. Many people consider being expected to examine a (possibly smudged) postmark to find the date the card was despatched irritating. Do not imitate this practice when you are writing your own postcards.

Postcards save time (because the message is only a few words long) and money (because although postage on cards and letters is the same the cost of a card is much less than that of writing paper and envelope). When they are completed in handwriting by the staff member concerned without going to the office for typing, further saving of time and money is achieved.

It is clear, however, that only certain simple communication situations can be adequately dealt with by postcards. It could seem lacking in courtesy to send a postcard for anything more than a routine reminder, acknowledgement, confirmation etc.

Exercise 53
Write two of the following postcards. To give you practice in spacing your message correctly on the card rule off an area $5\frac{1}{2}$ inches by $3\frac{1}{2}$ and write

within that. A firm's postcards will have a printed heading similar to that on their letter paper and you should allow for this in your layout.

(*a*) To a customer to tell her the item she has ordered is now ready for collection.

(*b*) To confirm that the hotel accommodation asked for has been reserved.

(*c*) To notify a client that Miss Elaine has left the salon and her appointment will therefore be with Miss Valerie.

(*d*) To remind a customer that her electric blanket is due for servicing and should be brought into the shop.

II. Reports

Reports normally arise under one of these situations:

1. Something has happened and you are required to say what you know about it – e.g. an *eye-witness account, accident report* etc.

2. You have been given certain work to do and are required to show how you are getting on with it – e.g. a *progress report*.

3. You have been instructed to look into a certain matter and now present your findings – e.g. an *examination report* (of an appliance for example), an *investigation report* etc.

If you were told to include your recommendations about what should be done about the matter investigated, your report becomes a *recommendatory report*.

The first type of report does not present any greater difficulty than any other communication situation. It is just a matter of making a clear statement about what you know. Such reports are often oral and quite informal – the boss simply says: 'Tell me exactly what happened', and you tell him. They sometimes, however, have to be prepared very carefully and written down with great exactness – if there is a question of an insurance claim or a legal action resulting. In this sort of report diagrams often play an important role in clarifying the physical relationships between the people and objects essential to the account. Exercise 54 provides some practice in preparing this kind of report.

Work reports normally present little problem.They are usually presented in a very simple form on predesigned forms which reduce the use of wording by the Tx to a minimum.

The third type of report is the most demanding but is not really likely to be asked for at work from users of this book for many years to come. If you are an officer of a club or society you may find you are required to present such a report, however. The exercises that follow are designed to introduce you to this sort of report so that you have some idea of how to tackle one if you are required to.

Exercise 54

Read this short report* through carefully. Then read the notes and instructions that follow it.

FARECO SUPERMARKETS

Preliminary Report on Jason-Howith
3B Incinerator

A. Terms of reference
On the instructions of the Chief Purchasing Officer (16 April 19..) a preliminary investigation into the suitability of Jason-Howith 3B incinerators for use in our supermarkets was carried out.

B. Procedure
1. Jason-Howith Ltd of Sparks Road, London, SE12 8JK were asked for full technical information on, and detailed specification of, their 3B incinerator.
2. All reports on file concerning the performance of all types of incinerator at present in use in our supermarkets were checked against this information.
3. Local authority clean air and fire precaution regulations in all areas where we have supermarkets were checked.

C. Design of incinerator
1. The incinerator is a complete disposal system in one compact unit, designed to handle wet and dry refuse, cartons, crates, rags, boxes, and similar items.
2. It is designed to operate unattended and the makers claim that inexperienced boy or girl employees can use it without risk of burns from flashback. When the charging door is opened, a controlled draught action pulls the fire away from the loading door and allows refuse or waste to be emptied into the incinerator without danger.

D. Performance of incinerator
1. The makers claim a high combustion efficiency (that for every 500 kg of combustible material burned one kg of dry sterile inorganic ash results).
2. It is claimed that the burner is smokeless at all times.

E. Conclusions
1. The incinerator meets the requirements of all relevant local authorities.
2. If the performance claimed is justified, the incinerator could cope with peak loading at all our supermarkets.
3. The method of operation, without the need to have an experienced employee attending to it regularly, meets the objection most commonly raised against all incinerators in present use.

* Adapted from a specimen report in Little: *English for the Office.*

F. Recommendations

One Jason-Howith 3B incinerator should be purchased, and installed at one of our London branches where its performance can be checked over a period under normal working conditions.

J. H. Traddle

27 April 19..

Notes

This report is written in what is sometimes called 'schematic' form – i.e. it is laid out in sections, using headings, lettering, numbering etc. to show the organisation of the material. We met this sort of thing before in Chapter 11 when we were looking at how to make notes. The report is not written in note form, however – it is in complete sentences throughout.

It is written *impersonally*. Thus we are told: *Local authority clean air and fire precaution regulations in all areas where we have supermarkets were checked*, not *I checked the local authority clean air and fire precaution regulations etc.* (first person form).

This is not the only way a short report can be written, although it is the usual method for a long or detailed report. Eye-witness reports (of accidents, for example) are always written in the first person, not impersonally. A report of the sort we are now examining could also have been written in the form of a letter from Traddle to the Chief Purchasing Officer. It would then have been written in the first person – i.e. Traddle would not be required to keep himself out of the report as he does in the impersonal schematic type of report.

In a report you should always make clear your terms of reference (i.e. who told you to investigate, and report on, what). This can be done in the introductory sentence of a report in letter form, or by a section specifically for this purpose at the start of a report in schematic form (as here).

Instructions

1. Rewrite the report in letter form, not using headings, numbering, or lettering.
2. Compare your version with the schematic version. Which do you consider the more satisfactory? Why?
3. What reasons can you think of for preferring the schematic form for longer or more detailed reports?

Exercise 55

Write a short report (about 150 words) on an accident at your place of work that occurs to either a colleague or a customer. This can be in either schematic or letter form.

Exercise 56

Business has been falling off at the shop/store/salon/restaurant/hotel you work at. The manager has invited any junior member of staff who thinks he/she can suggest reasons for this, and ways in which the situation can be improved, to submit a memorandum to him.

NOTE. A 'memorandum' is much the same as a report but it has no terms of reference section defining who instructed you to make the report because you are not *instructed* to submit a memorandum – you put in a memorandum because you want to (or think you ought to).

Either inventing all details or basing your material upon your actual experiences at work, write out your memorandum. This should be at least 200 words long.

Exercise 57
Write one of the following short reports (about 300 words). Invent all details (including names and addresses) necessary to make your report seem real.

(a) You have been instructed by the chairman of the students' union to prepare a report on the college refectory giving particular attention to these points: (1) How can students be served more quickly? (2) How can waste of food be avoided?

(b) You are secretary of a youth organisation. A local business man has offered you rather dilapidated premises (a wooden hut) for a rent of £12 per annum. You have been instructed by the executive committee to prepare a report on the suitability of these premises for your organisation's use and to advise whether the offer should be accepted.

(c) You are an area supervisor for a small chain of grocers. All but one of your firm's shops are now self-service. You visit this last shop and report on its suitability for conversion to self-service and whether you recommend this.

III. What shopkeepers and shop assistants think of customers

The following letters are a selection from a group published in *Which*. If you work in a shop you will be particularly interested in what the writers have to say. When you have read them through there are some questions to answer about them.

1. By saying how useful and interesting it would be if assistants or shopkeepers wrote to let you know what *we* think of customers – you have really cut yourself a piece of cake! As an employer, I see faults in my own assistants which I attempt to eradicate – unfortunately one cannot take the same attitude with our customers. Many of these practise dishonest little tricks – not by stealing but in their attempts to put one over on the assistant, and thereby ultimately on the shopkeeper. They are price conscious to the exclusion of the value or services they are receiving in exchange for their money; and many tell petty lies. Many of those who shout loudest at any increases in the price of goods or services are the very ones who will strike for a rise in wages for themselves, but they are

too short-sighted to see the spiral. Ideally there should be classes where employers, assistants and customers could hear each other's points of view and endeavour to meet each other at least half way.

O. M., Solihull, Warwicks

2. Customers – never have I known so many unreasonable, rude, irresponsible and dishonest people. They are after their 'rights' which are being drummed into them, but they do not know their 'responsibilities'.

G. H. V., Ilfracombe, N. Devon

3. Please don't start off with 'I know you won't have . . .' Why ask if you know we won't have it? Also do not handle food and please remove your gloves before you look at books or paper goods. Your gloves are dirtier than you think and bend the edges of paper goods making them look not quite new. You are quite within your rights in refusing soiled goods so remember who soils them.

W. T., Cheshire

4. Do not bring your children into a store and allow them to run wild among thousands of pounds worth of goods. The smallest mark on, say, a table or refrigerator will lower its value by pounds. Do not expect an assistant to greet you with enthusiasm at closing time. He has been on his feet serving hundreds of people all day and is longing to get home to his family. He is only human, not a serving machine.

T. J., Sidcup, Kent

5. It is true to say that a large proportion of the public are offensive to the shop assistants. Their attitude is, one imagines, somewhat similar to that shown to domestics during the reign of Victoria. This attitude is not confined to the upper classes. The newly affluent working class are equally overbearing. The fact remains, however, that working behind the counter is a despised occupation and this conception will remain, until the status of the shop assistant is raised and the job carries some standing in the public eye.

Retailer

6. Shop assistants must be the last bastions of servitude remaining; we are treated by the majority of middle-class customers as the domestics were treated 50 years ago. Most customers are curt and many rude yet we dare not defend ourselves or answer back. I should be horrified to see my own children in such a humiliating job. Thank goodness they are better equipped with degrees than I was.

I. H.

7. Customers simply stare at the assistant without making any reply, others merely 'sniff' audibly. Two or three such encounters will daunt even the most courageous and carefully trained assistant until, small wonder, they will only speak when spoken to and then

without a smile. Complaining, on the part of the customer, has become something of a disease. Few customers are able to complain lucidly and to good effect because their motives, generally, are not to right a wrong but to get an assistant into trouble or to get something for nothing.

H. W., Sheffield, Yorks

8. The It's-not-for-me type enquires after an item in which I can show the most comprehensive range possible. Wastes up to half an hour of my time but parts with the words 'I'll tell my sister (brother, mother, father, daughter, etc.) you've got it'. Please don't prevaricate, we usually can tell and it really isn't necessary.

G. S., Hove, Sussex

Questions

Letter 1
(*a*) Is the writer a shopkeeper or a shop assistant?
(*b*) What do you think the author means by the following expressions: *cut yourself a piece of cake; attempts to put one over on the assistant; price conscious to the exclusion of the value or services they are receiving; the spiral*? Would you consider any of these expressions colloquial?
(*c*) What is the meaning, as used in the letter, of *eradicate; practise; ultimately; petty.*
(*d*) Can you suggest a better punctuation for the first sentence?

Letter 2
(*a*) What is the difference between *rights* and *responsibilities*?
(*b*) Why, do you imagine, does the writer put these words between inverted commas?
(*c*) What does *irresponsible* mean?

Letter 3
(*a*) Do you think the writer was correct in using *Also* to start the second paragraph of this letter?
(*b*) Can you suggest a better punctuation for the last sentence?

Letter 4
What two points are made in this letter?

Letter 5
What is the meaning, as used in the letter, of *domestics, affluent, overbearing, conception, status*?

Letter 6
(*a*) What is a *bastion*? Although one can see what the writer means by the expression *bastions of servitude* there is something unsatisfactory about his use of it – what?
(*b*) What is the meaning, as used in the letter, of *curt; humiliating*?

Letter 7
(*a*) What two points are made in this letter?
(*b*) What is the meaning, as used in the letter, of *audibly, daunt, lucidly*?

Letter 8
(*a*) What is the meaning, as used in the letter, of *comprehensive, prevaricate*?
(*b*) What is the writer really objecting to in this letter?

Exercise 58
Write a magazine article of 200 words entitled *The Shop Assistant's View of the Customer*. You may use both your own experience and points raised in these letters.

IV. Additional practice work

Exercise 59
You are hoping to sell your car by means of a classified advertisement in the local newpaper. Here is a check list of points it is desirable to include:

Make
Model
Year
Colour
Taxed until
Number of owners
Mileage (original or on new engine)
Recent new parts (including tyres, suspension, gearbox, battery, dynamo)
If regularly serviced
Price
Telephone number and address
Time/s when car can be seen

You cannot include all these because the amount you are prepared to pay for your advertisement will buy you only 40 words, to include two lines (of one to four words in length) which will be printed in 'bold face' (heavy black) type. Decide which are the most important details to include (inventing these if you do not own a car) and write out your advertisement as you wish it to appear, indicating your bold face lines by double underlining.

Exercise 60
Before you could sell your car you were involved in a collision with another vehicle and have now to claim on your insurance company. Invent sufficient details of the accident to enable you to complete the part of your company's claim form printed opposite. Do not attempt to write on the form – the sections are numbered and you should write out each entry under its number, on a separate sheet of paper.

1. Plan of accident   showing road signs, if any, estimated measurements
                                of road, and position of vehicles; if no signs, indicate
                                relative importance of roads

2. Description of accident

....

....

....

....

....

....

....

....

....

3. If the road is subject to speed limit, give details...

....

4. Speed (a) immediately before impact ....(b) on impact ....

5. What was the state of (a) the weather?..........................(b) the road?...........................

6. Details of damage to insured vehicle and estimated cost of repair.................................

....

....

Exercise 61

An enquiry into shoppers' preferences carried out in two towns (Norwich
and Stevenage) revealed the points listed on p. 170. They are not put down
in a very logical order and, because they are repetitive and poorly
organised, are difficult to follow.

Your task is (*a*) to make sure you understand the points made, and (*b*)
to rearrange the material and present it in a way that an Rx rather like

yourself in age and educational background who was working in retailing and hoped to be accepted for training as an under-manager would find easy to follow. You may use either well laid out notes or continuous prose.

1. Supermarkets are thought to give good value for money and good variety of groceries.
2. Elderly people prefer small local shops.
3. Shoppers favour Friday and Saturday for food purchasing.
4. Shoppers require parking at shopping centre.
5. Traffic-free streets or precincts are favoured.
6. People enjoy using supermarkets.
7. Mothers with young children like local shops.
8. Mothers would pay to have children under five looked after at shops while they themselves are shopping.
9. Covered pavements for shopping areas are liked.
10. Shops on one level are preferred.
11. A town centre should not be windy.
12. Parking on one level is preferred.
13. If stores are on more than one level, lavatories, food, and women's and children's clothing should be on the ground floor.
14. Groceries are thought to be cheaper at supermarkets.
15. People appreciate beautiful surroundings in their shopping centre.
16. What people want most in a shopping centre is a large variety of shops.
17. Parking should be on one level.
18. The shopping area should include lavatories, phone boxes, and seating.
19. Shoppers do not plan their weekly food purchasing ahead.

Exercise 62
With the aid of the information given, write an article of about 300 words entitled 'Young people as a market'.

Here are some points to think about before you start.

How are you going to organise your material? The facts that you are given are (deliberately) very poorly arranged. Remember what you learned in Part One about organisation and paragraphing.

Why is there so much stress on newspapers, TV and the cinema? What have these to do with selling to young people?

The information supplied gives little help with starting and finishing your article. Can you think out a sentence or two of your own to supply an introduction and a conclusion?

1. Young people may be defined as the 10 – 34 year-olds.
2. Young people account for three-quarters of all cinema admissions.
3. The 16 – 24 age group buy 70 per cent of all motor scooters sold.
4. The smallest proportion of heavy viewing of TV is amongst the 16 – 24 age group.
5. Young people number 9.9 million males, 9.6 million females.
6. Young people comprise 34.7 per cent of the total population.
7. Teenagers account for 10.3 per cent of annual spending on confectionery.

8. Young men attend the cinema more frequently than girls.
9. Young people with more money to spend watch TV less than those with less to spend.
10. Young people will be 37 per cent of the population by year 2000.
11. Only 7 per cent of unmarried 16 – 24 year olds are heavy TV viewers.
12. There has been an increase of 24 per cent in cinema going amongst the 16 – 24 age group.
13. 25 per cent of all housewives are 'young people'.
14. Teenagers account for 15 per cent of all money spent on clothing annually.
15. The 16 – 24 age group spends £35 million a year on toiletries and cosmetics.
16. 19.2 per cent of all money spent on footwear is spent by teenagers.
17. Young households spend above the average on drink, tobacco, clothing, footwear, durables, transport, and vehicles.
18. Teenage girls buy magazines regularly.
19. Teenagers account for 11.6 per cent of all money spent annually on meals, snacks, and soft drinks.
20. In 1970 savings amongst unmarried 16 – 24 year-olds totalled about £140 million.
21. 18.4 per cent of all spending on dancing and cinemas is by teenagers.
22. Few teenagers buy newspapers.
23. There has been a rise of 24 per cent in cinema going in the 16 – 24 age group.
24. Young households spend less than the average on fuel, food, and services.
25. One third of all U.K. holiday makers abroad are aged 16 – 24.

Appendix 1: Spelling

English spelling is very confusing and it is not surprising that most people make a few mistakes from time to time. The trouble is that we have no consistent system by which a certain letter, or group of letters, always equals the one sound. Or, putting this the other way round, we have several ways of spelling the same sound. Think of *way, whey, made, maid,* – four ways of spelling the *a* sound, and the first word and the second, the third word and the fourth sound exactly alike although spelled differently. An outstanding example is the combination *ough*, used to spell so many sounds – e.g. *thought, though, rough, cough, bough, borough*.

Although occasional mistakes are therefore understandable enough, they can nevertheless do considerable harm to you and your firm. If, for example, you put up a handwritten notice that has a spelling mistake in it, this will make a very unfortunate impression on customers. At the least it makes you (and your firm) look careless – since you could have checked the spelling in a dictionary.

Really bad spellers – those whose spelling makes it difficult for the Rx even to guess what words are intended – may fail to communicate altogether.

Very few people feel 100 per cent confident about their spelling; almost everybody is aware of the need to improve it. The hints that follow are a little indigestible if taken at one gulp. Referred to from time to time, however, as difficulties occur, they will gradually produce lasting improvements – especially if supported by increased reading.

Most spelling errors come under one of the three following headings.

1. ERRORS OF MEMORY

You just cannot remember whether it is *ie* or *ei* in certain words; whether a plural is *ies* or *ys;* whether the ending is *ible* or *able* etc. The most widespread uncertainty of this kind is over whether certain words are spelled with a double or a single consonant (e.g. *parallel, guarantee, occasion, embarrassment*).

Some of these points are dealt with in the rules that follow below. For the rest it is a matter of learning by heart words you frequently misspell. If you have a blind spot over a certain word you should try to memorise the spelling when you look it up in the dictionary – otherwise you will find yourself looking up the same word week after week.

2. ERRORS OF MISUNDERSTANDING

These occur when there are two or more spellings (with differing meanings) for words that sound alike (e.g. *their, there, they're*). Such words are dealt with in some detail on page 125.

3. BASIC ERRORS

These are errors in simple everyday words where there is no element of confusion as in the first two categories. If you are a bad speller of this kind you may even spell the same word several ways in the one piece of writing. Sometimes the misspelling is caused by a speech fault (e.g. *as* for *has* and vice versa). Misspelling of this kind is usually the result of lack of reading and can be put right only by doing a lot of reading. Unfortunately, if you are this sort of bad speller you are probably a poor reader too and find it really hard work to do much reading – but that is the only way to improve.

Some spelling rules

RULE ONE. *i* before *e* except after *c* (where the sound is as in *piece*).
  Exceptions: *counterfeit, Keith, seize, Sheila, weir, weird.*

RULE TWO. In compounds the *ll* of *all, full, fill, till, well* becomes *l*. Thus *almighty, fulfil, handful, until, welfare.*

  Exceptions: *farewell, illness, tallness, smallness, wellbeing.*

RULE THREE. One-syllable words ending in vowel and single consonant double the consonant when *ed, ing* or *er* is added. Thus *run, running,* but *grunt, grunting.*
  One-syllable words ending in vowel, single consonant, and silent *e* do not double the consonant when *ed, ing* or *er* is added. Thus *plan, planning,* but *plane, planing; fin, finned,* but *fine, fined.*
  Words of more than one syllable behave similarly *except when there is no stress on the final syllable* (*profit, profiting*).
  Exception: *worship, worshipping.*

RULE FOUR. In compounds, silent *e* is retained before a consonant, dropped before a vowel. Thus *lively,* but *living, valueless* but *valuable.*
  Exceptions: *argument, awful, duly, truly, unduly, wholly, wisdom.*

NOTE. Before *a o* or *u* the *e* is retained after *g* or *c* to indicate that the *g* or *c* is 'soft' in pronunciation. Thus *managing* but *manageable.*

RULE FIVE. Nouns ending in *y* form their plurals by adding *ies* – except where the *y* is preceded by a vowel. Thus *penny, pennies* but *chimney, chimneys.*

Appendix 2:
The Post Office Alphabet

This alphabet was designed originally for use when spelling out words over the telephone. It also has its uses face-to-face. Initials and letter codes can be difficult to distinguish even at quite close quarters and we use a great many of them these days. Thus 'You will have to complete a PD4' can be heard as *You will have to complete a BD4*. If you say 'PD4, Peter David 4' there is no confusion.

Of course, other words and names can be, and are, used, but this alphabet has two advantages: 1. it has been carefully compiled to avoid any two words that sound in any way alike; 2. a very large number of people know it by heart. You would be well advised to join them, if you use the telephone much in your work.

A	for Alfred	J	for Jack	S	for Samuel
B	for Benjamin	K	for King	T	for Tommy
C	for Charlie	L	for London	U	for Uncle
D	for David	M	for Mary	V	for Victor
E	for Edward	N	for Nellie	W	for William
F	for Frederick	O	for Oliver	X	for X-Ray
G	for George	P	for Peter	Y	for Yellow
H	for Harry	Q	for Queen	Z	for Zebra.
I	for Isaac	R	for Robert		

Appendix 3: Postcodes

The Post Office has been, over the past few years, gradually introducing a system of postcodes (public postal address codes) that will eventually cover all the country. The postcode is a condensed form of the address information needed for sorting a letter at each stage of its journey to the postman who is going to deliver it. By encoding the information it is possible to convert it into a pattern of dots that can be 'read' by sorting machines.

The postcode is in two halves. The first (or 'outward') half consists of letters (or a single letter) followed by a number. The letters identify the 'post town'; the number may indicate a smaller town within the area of the post town, or a district of the post town. The second (or 'inward') half of the postcode consists of a figure from 0 to 9 followed by two letters. This may identify a street, part of a street, even an individual address if it is one where more than twenty letters are normally received by the first delivery.

In the example CF6 2PR, *CF6* is the outward half, *2PR* the inward half. *CF* identifies the post town (Cardiff), *6* a small town (Barry), *2PR* a specific very small area of Barry, where the letter is to be delivered.

For efficient working of automatic sorting, and to avoid delay in delivery of letters, it will be necessary to show postcodes as part of the address on envelopes. To ensure that letters sent to them are correctly postcoded, firms will have to incorporate their postcodes into their letter headings, and most firms have been doing this as soon as their postcodes were received. Similarly, people writing from private addresses will have to remember to include their postcodes with their addresses. Undoubtedly, it will also become the custom to include the postcode with the inside address of a business letter, as shown in the examples in this book.

For all these applications the following rules, based upon Post Office suggestions, should be observed:

1. Make the postcode the last item of the address. Preferably it should be on a separate line; if it has to share a line with other information it should be separated from this by at least the width of two characters in handwriting or two spaces on a typewriter.

2. If you consider that by placing the postcode on a line by itself will make the address take up too much space, put the county on the same line as the post town.
3. Separate the two halves of the postcode by a space the width of one character in handwriting or one space on a typewriter.
4. In handwriting, use block capitals for the letters of the postcode. On a typewriter use upper case.
5. Do not join the characters of the postcode in any way.
6. Do not use full stops or other punctuations with the postcode.
7. Do not underline the postcode.

Appendix 4:
A Metrication Guide

	Unit	Symbol	Comment
1. LENGTH	metre	m	
	millimetre	mm	0·001 m
	kilometre	km	1 000 m
2. AREA	square metre	m^2 or sq m	
	hectare	ha	100 m x 100 m
3. VOLUME	cubic metre	m^3 or cu m	
	cubic millimetre	mm^3	
4. CAPACITY	litre	l	
5. WEIGHT	gramme	g	
	kilogramme	kg	
	tonne	t	
6. TIME	second	s	
7. VELOCITY	metre per second	m/s	
8. TEMPERATURE	degree Celsius	°C	approved name for 'Centigrade'
9. ELECTRICITY			
(current)	ampere	A	
(potential)	volt	V	
10. POWER	watt	W	
	kilowatt	kW	
11. PREFIXES	mega	M	1 000 000
	kilo	k	1 000
	hecto	h	100
	deca	da	10
	deci	d	0.1
	centi	c	0·01
	milli	m	0·001
	micro	μ	0·000 000 1

NOTE
1. Do not put a full stop after a symbol (except to mark the end of a sentence).

2. The same symbol is used for both singular and plural.
3. The type case of the symbol (i.e. capital letter or not) must be as above – particularly important in distinguishing *mega* (M) from *milli* (m).
4. Do not hyphenate units based on a prefix (NOT *milli-metre*).
5. Do not use a comma to mark off thousands. For numerals *more than four figures long* a space should be used instead to indicate thousands and millions.
6. Always use 0 before the decimal point when the quantity is less than one.
7. Whole numbers should be given without a following decimal point.
8. Do not mix units (*20.75 kg* NOT *20 kg 75 g*).
9. Always write the unit in full if there is the slightest chance that use of the symbol will cause misunderstanding.